ABANDONED NOT
BROKEN

The PASSION & PERSPECTIVE
to discover your PURPOSE

ABANDONED NOT
BROKEN

The PASSION & PERSPECTIVE
to discover your PURPOSE

ROB JOHNSON

XULON PRESS ELITE

Xulon Press Elite
2301 Lucien Way #415
Maitland, FL 32751
407.339.4217
www.xulonpress.com

Unless otherwise indicated, Scripture quotations taken from the English Standard Version (ESV). Copyright © 2001 by Crossway, a publishing ministry of Good News Publishers. Used by permission. All rights reserved.

Paperback ISBN-13: 978-1-6312-9995-7

Ebook ISBN-13: 978-1-6312-9996-4

DEDICATION

Who knows where I would be and what would have happened if Pat Johnson (my only mother) didn't accept to raise me as her own? I know it wasn't easy, but you never let us see you sweat. I owe my life to you! No words can describe how much I love you! Thank You, Thank You, Thank You!

My wife and kids are the reason I work so hard to be a better me every day. Heather, from the day I said, "I do", I promised to love you through thick and thin til death do us part. That vow continues to ring true each and every day I wake up. I couldn't imagine life without you by my side. You have blessed me with three amazing children. I could never begin to repay you for your daily sacrifices to keep it all together.

Ky, Kenz and Dallas thanks for making me a proud dad. Each one of you are special in your own way. Stay unique and work hard to become whatever you put your mind to! You guys make life worth it.

CONTENTS

ACKNOWLEDGMENTS

Thank you, Tonia and Brian, for never making me feel like I didn't belong. The best sister and brother a guy could ask for. Thanks for allowing me to become "mom's favorite"!

A special thank you to my Aunt Diane and Uncle Wayne. You guys made sure I always had what I needed growing up from Christmas and birthdays to everyday in between. You were always there to help my mom when times were tough. I will never forget all the weekend sleepovers and family parties' you guys hosted. You are two very special human beings that will forever be in my heart.

Through the years I watched my Aunt Doris go without so she could give my cousin Amber the world. Aunt Doris is the most caring, unselfish person I've ever met. Her faith in God continuously encourages me to keep my faith as well. Thank you for loving me and my family unconditionally!

Thanks to all my Bridgeton Assembly of God family for loving me as your own. You came along and helped my mom anyway you could. It really does take a village. Forever grateful to you all.

Thanks, Shelton Joyner, for being my brother from another mother. We have been there for each other through good times and bad. There will never be another "Ebony and Ivory"!

Thanks Nanny and Poppop for being the most awesome grandparents to ever live. Life hasn't been the same without you. I hope I'm making you proud.

Pastor Ryan and family at Lakewood Chapel, thanks for helping me continue to grow my relationship with God. My life has changed so much since attending the church. God is on the move and I'm glad to serve alongside you all.

Thanks, Reggie, for helping me from the start. I appreciate you and your ability to bring my ideas to life.

FOREWORD

A few months ago, when I was spending time at Rob's house, he shared with me the very exciting news that he would be writing a book about his life story. I was immediately excited to hear this because I knew enough of his story to know just how much of an impact his story would have on anyone that would pick up his book and read it. When Rob asked me to write the foreword for his book, I was extremely honored because I've been blessed to know Rob for the past six years not only as his pastor but also as one of my closest friends.

One of the things that I admire most about Rob is how big his heart is for others. It always inspires and encourages me to witness the success that Rob experiences in life because he immediately gives the credit to God and always looks for a way to turn every success he has into a blessing for someone else, especially those who are hurting and less fortunate. He truly embodies the words of Jesus found in Matthew 25:34-40:

> Then the King will say to those on his right,
> 'Come, you who are blessed by my Father,
> inherit the kingdom prepared for you from
> the foundation of the world. For I was

hungry and you gave me food, I was thirsty and you gave me drink, I was a stranger and you welcomed me, I was naked and you clothed me, I was sick and you visited me, I was in prison and you came to me.' Then the righteous will answer him, saying, 'Lord, when did we see you hungry and feed you, or thirsty and give you drink? And when did we see you a stranger and welcome you, or naked and clothe you? And when did we see you sick or in prison and visit you?' And the King will answer them, 'Truly, I say to you, as you did it to one of the least of these my brothers, you did it to me.'

I have seen his heart be touched not just for people in his life, but even for those he has yet to meet, he gladly extends his generosity to all. It's this incredible heart and passion that Rob has that has made it such a blessing to be his friend as well as to have him serve as such an important leader in our church. I cannot think of a better person to write a book with the title *Abandoned Not Broken* than Rob Johnson, because even though his life story might start with being abandoned and faced with many difficult times and trials in his life, he is definitely not broken. He clearly shows that His Father in heaven has picked up the pieces Satan has so desperately tried to shatter and that God has had

His hand upon His life "to work all things together for good" (Romans 8:28).

In this book, Rob gives his readers an inspirational example from his own life story of the purpose that you can find in life when you choose to place your faith in Jesus Christ— no matter what pain, disappointment, or failures exist in your life. No matter what your story is or where you find yourself at in life, when you read *Abandoned Not Broken,* you will be inspired to have the passion and perspective you need to discover your purpose!

Rev. Ryan Atkinson
Pastor at Lakewood Chapel

INTRODUCTION

Why is it always someone else's fault that you turned out the way you did? You're right, passing the blame onto someone is easier than facing the man in the mirror. We often use our past as a crutch as to why we can't succeed in life. Our level of self-worth seems to diminish during times of trouble in our lives. I'm pretty sure we would all have preferred to be born to the perfect family, with tons of money and fame. Trust me, that comes with its own set of problems. I'm actually glad to have been born to a mother who wasn't ready to be a mom. Without my biological mom and dad, I wouldn't be here today.

Life is what you make it! I could have spent my whole life being upset that I was given up for adoption. I know this sounds crazy, but I'm actually grateful that my biological mother realized she couldn't give me a good life and chose to allow someone who could raise me instead. Throughout my life, obstacles would keep coming my way from being raised without a dad to being teased or made fun of for having a black sister, it was up to me how I would handle it.

I can remember actually getting into fights for people using racial slurs while talking about my sister. Growing up we pretty much had what we needed but we didn't always have what we wanted. You learned to be happy with what you got and didn't get upset. However, I would often wonder "Why me? Why do I have to go through life this way?" As I grew older, I realized I wanted more for my life and if I wanted something, I had to work for it. They say hard work pays off!

For me, high school just wasn't something I wanted to work for, and I ended up dropping out and getting my GED. While most people stay in school and take the education route, I chose not to. Some days I wish I had the chance to do it all over again. It was a hard-long road for me and throughout my journey you will see all that life throws at me. Through it all God had a perfect plan for my life when I had not a clue.

Knowing that I could do anything, I put my mind to it. I had to focus on my tomorrow. So many people need to know that regardless of what they faced yesterday, tomorrow is a new day. We have the power to let our past make or break us. I chose to use my past to empower myself to set big goals and work very hard to accomplish them. Along the way, I had special people help keep me focused.

Oftentimes, I find myself encouraging young people in my community to keep pushing. You should never forget where you came from yet never stop pushing to be better. I like to share my story to help others understand that no matter what, anything is possible. Almost every time I share my story with someone they respond with, "you should write a book." I honestly never felt like I had a book worthy story until one day God spoke to me. At that moment, I realized if one person can receive the gift of Hope through my story it's worth me writing a book.

Regardless of what my yesterday looked like, you will be able to see how I handled life's obstacles throughout this book. I often get a chance to speak to people throughout my community that don't know how they will face their tomorrow. I answer them simply by saying this, "You have to change the YOU inside, no one can change who you are. It's all about your perspective."

We all have the power to not allow our past to dictate our future. I may have been abandoned; however, I chose not to let it break me!

What real love looks like.

Chapter 1

BORN A DUNCKLEY

Red hair, pale face, covered in freckles from head to toe. She was very friendly, well-mannered and loved by all who knew her. What's not to love? To the human eye, she was young, beautiful and full of life. These are all words people have used to describe Janie.

One day, while visiting a local liquor store, she met a young man named Gary. They hit it off almost instantly. Before long, the two were more than just strangers in a store. Janie knew she finally found her true love. She thought this was the one who just might change her life. In just a few short months, Gary informed Janie that he would be relocating for work. Soon after Gary left town, Janie realized something that would once again change her life.

Day after day, all she could think about was the fact that she wasn't ready to be a mother again! This would be her third time carrying a child. Considering the fact that her first two children were already being raised by an immediate family member, she knew this pregnancy would be much different. Her family could not afford nor were they willing to take on caring for another child. What would she do?

On Wednesday, August 15, 1979, a little boy was born. What an exciting moment for his parents, well for most parents anyway. "What's his name?" the medical team asked? "Robert Thomas Dunckley" she replied. After confirmation that no one in her family would take the little boy, she decided it was up to her to try to do whatever she could to make it work.

With little to no resources or help from family because they wanted no parts of it, she was left feeling all alone with this newborn baby boy and had nowhere to go. With the "so-called" father out of the picture now as well, Janie was the only thing left in this kid's life. The one saving grace Janie had left was her great-grandmother. Being that she was in her 80s, she couldn't offer to help raise the child but she would often assist to find child care and pay for it so Janie could work and try to make somewhat of a life for her and this child.

Ms. Hepner, the great grandmother, had owned a few rental properties throughout the town and had a great relationship with her tenants. One in particular was by far her favorite. Ms. Hepner knew that this lady watched kids and was an overall great person. She thought Janie would be very pleased to have her son looked after by someone she adored so greatly. Janie was happy to receive any help at all. Having a newborn and raising him alone was honestly not what Janie had in mind for her life. It was way more work than she had ever expected, and it didn't help that the little boy would begin to show signs of medical issues.

Within a few days of learning of this awesome babysitter, Janie had finally made arrangements to drop the baby boy off. Miss Pat, who was the babysitter, was so excited to be watching a newborn baby. Never did she think she would be handed a child who was soaked through his clothes and smelled horrendous. She began to change the little guy and immediately noticed signs of neglect. The cloth diaper he was wearing had started to grow into his skin. She knew right away that he needed to be seen by a doctor sooner rather than later. She eagerly waited for the mother to return so she could tell her about what she saw.

Before Miss Pat knew it, days had gone by without a trace of the little boy's mother. Miss Pat took it upon herself to make a doctor's appointment for the baby in order for him to be treated for his sickness which ended up being a blood infection. With only being able to communicate with the great-grandmother, Miss Pat had figured that this may be Janie's' way of just walking away from her child. Over a month had passed with only constant conversations with the great grand-mother, who informed Miss Pat that she would love for her to raise the little boy as her own. Miss Pat would reach out to the Division of Family Services to get the ball rolling on making that a reality.

Already being a single mother of two other children, Pat was not new to motherhood and she welcomed "Robbie" into her home as one of her own. She would continue to love him just as she did her biological children. Though their last names were different, her love for Robbie was the same as it was for the two children who shared her last name. Eventually, months later, Janie would reach out to Pat to try and explain her reasoning for leaving. She was overwhelmed and just could not possibly raise this little boy. Janie was pleased that Pat was willing to raise Robbie as her own.

Janie would call and visit from time to time, even referring to herself as mommy, mom, or mother. Little did she know, she would always just be Janie to me. I already had a mom who loved me very much. For me, there was just no room for Janie and honestly, I was still too young to understand the relationship.

Throughout the years, there would be weekly visits with the case workers from DYFS. These workers would take me to McDonald's, out to buy a small toy or even a simple ice cream cone. Every time, without fail, I would be asked if I liked where I was living? Questions such as: "Do you feel loved?" and "Are you happy to be in that house?" became standard conversation during these visits. My answer would always remain the same, "Yes! Yes! Yes!" My new family was awesome, and I loved it there. I would often say, "Even though I am a Dunckley, they make me feel like a Johnson."

An innocent young boy who had no idea of the reality of his troubled beginning.

I was a happy kid who loved my "new" family just as much as they loved me.

Chapter 2

LIFE AS A JOHNSON

The day began like every other normal school day. The bus ride was noisy and rowdy as usual. After getting off the bus, it was time to grab a little breakfast from the cafeteria before heading upstairs to Room #6, Mrs. Letterman's class. She was my second-grade teacher.

My desk was pretty close to the front because the seating was arranged in alphabetical order by last name. I was still a Dunckley at this point. I can remember being so excited to get out of school early that day however, if I'm being honest, I was pretty nervous. I wasn't sure what to expect once I had left school for the day.

After a brief car ride, we finally arrived at the Cumberland County Courthouse. My nerves had me feeling queasy. I wasn't quite sure what was going to take place exactly. Soon after arriving, I was greeted by my favorite case worker. I remember going into a small room with just my case worker and a Judge, talk about nerve racking! The Judge asked me a few questions to see how I was doing. Questions such as "Do you know why you're here today? How is school going for you? What grade are you in? How do you like living with Pat? What do you think about Brian and Tonia?" Talk about intense!

Once we finished in that tiny room, I was brought into the big courtroom where my foster mom Pat was sitting. Just a tad overwhelming for a young boy. I could see the tears running down Pat's face as she wiped them away with a tissue. "Oh no, are they not going to let her be my mom?" The Judge walked out wearing a big black robe and sat behind the stand facing the courtroom. He began speaking about how important it was to learn how to love and care for each other. He also spoke about how adoptions work and what that responsibility entails. He said some very nice things about my foster mom and how lucky of a little boy I was. "Phew, I think this is going well!" I thought, relieved by his words.

"Young man, after talking to you, your caseworker and Pat, it sounds like you are one lucky kid." Even this man, who knew only what my files said and what was discussed between us that day, realized the same thing that I did. How amazing was it that someone who didn't have to love me nor like me, decided that she would not only love me but call me her son? I was on cloud nine and the butterflies in my stomach were starting to flutter for all the right reasons.

The best part of the entire day was about to occur. The Judge called us up front to stand. He began to speak again and told me to repeat after him. The same was asked of Pat. When this part was finished, all you heard was the sound of his gavel hitting the wood. "Young man, you are now officially a Johnson, give your mom a hug." I was so happy to finally have a family I could call my own. I'll never forget that day or the sacrifices Pat made to welcome me into her family with open arms. She is the true hero in this story!

My permanent family, myself, my mom Pat, my sister Tonia and my brother Brian. They have never made me feel anything less than family.

My next day at school was just a little bit different. Because of all the alphabetical seating charts, I just about changed my seat in every class I was in as well as where I would stand in line. These changes reminded me of one thing, the best day of my life, becoming a Johnson!

Pat is now the single mother of three children raising a blended family. Some may question why she would even think to put herself through that. This wouldn't be the first obstacle in raising a family that she had faced. As interracial dating let alone marriage was frowned up during the birth of her first child, Pat was used to fighting for what she believed in and this was no obstacle she couldn't conquer.

Tonia is the oldest and only daughter; her father and Pat were married for a short time then divorced.

Brian is the middle son and then there is me, now known to my family as Robbie, the baby boy. Being that Tonia was ten years older, she was able to help out around the house. My mom worked a few different jobs to make ends meet. We lived in Tips Trailer Park in Bridgeton, New Jersey. This would be my home for my entire childhood.

There wasn't a day that went by that something would happen to upset my mom. No matter how much she worked or sacrificed, it never seemed to be enough. My aunt and uncle or my grandparents would always come to our rescue. I can still see my mom in the kitchen preparing a meal for us on a hot plate because she couldn't afford the gas or propane needed for the appliances.

We always had hand me downs in our house. We weren't picky, we were just grateful to have something. Our trailer only consisted of two bedrooms. Tonia had one room to herself because she was the oldest and only girl. My mom had the back bedroom which was tiny with little room to spare. This room held my mom's clothes as well as mine and my brother Brian's. The dryer was also located in this tiny room.

My brother would sleep on the couch most nights and I would sleep on the floor in the living room. If I was lucky, some nights I would fall asleep on the couch before my brother got home. When this happened, my mom would sleep on the recliner and let my brother sleep in the back bedroom. I know what you're probably thinking, "Why in the world would they let her adopt him if she didn't have room for him?" Though this doesn't sound like an ideal situation, I surely was loved and cared for and these circumstances are part of what helped shaped me.

Cable was just not in the budget, UHF and VHF was about all we could get. I still remember being the personal remote control. I would have to walk up to the 13-inch tv, move the antennae and turn the knobs back and forth until a show would come in clear enough for mom to see.

We never really had the opportunity to have many of the things that we wanted, however, our mom always seemed to give us exactly what we needed. To this day, I'm still not quite sure how she pulled it all off. As I got older, I began to recognize the sacrifices my mom made for us. I remember the phone being shut off more days than it was on. Notes of being evicted would be taped to our door as I arrived home from school. Regardless of what my mom had to do, she never quit. Seeing that fight in her all those years ago helped me become who I am today and taught me some very valuable lessons!

Chapter 3

A MEDICAL MISHAP

While working numerous jobs to keep the bills paid, my mom decided to get weight loss surgery in an attempt to better her health. Gastric Bypass Surgery was very new to the medical field; now it's trending across the globe. The doctor was convinced that my mom was the perfect candidate for the surgery. At this time, I was only 9 years old. My mom was so excited to finally have the opportunity to lose weight and live a much happier, healthier life. Being the nervous little guy that I was, I was extremely scared for her to get the procedure done.

The day finally came, and my mom woke us all up to say goodbye before she headed to the hospital. It was a day I would never forget. I tried to convince her to let me stay home from school with my sister. She was not having it and insisted that I needed to be at school. She promised that I would be able to see her as soon as school was over.

During the day at school I felt so overwhelmed with nerves and anxiety. I had a difficult time concentrating on my schoolwork. My teachers were aware of my mom's surgery and encouraged me throughout the day that everything would be just fine. I was not fine though, in fact all the worrying landed me in the Nurse's office feeling nauseous.

After a long and exhausting day at school, the bus ride home seemed like it took forever. We finally arrived at the big, dusty, bus stop in front of Tips Trailer Park in Bridgeton, New Jersey. Waiting for me outside of the bus was my Aunt Diane. This is the same aunt who often came to our rescue whenever we needed anything. We went and visited my grandparents while we waited to hear about how my mom's surgery went. Not long after arriving, the phone rang and my grandmom answered. Just the tone of her voice made me think something wasn't right. Soon after she hung up the phone, she and my aunt rushed out of the house to go to the hospital while I stayed back with my poppop.

My poppop reassured me that my mom was just fine. I never ended up seeing my mom that day. I was sent home with my sister and brother and was told that I would be able to go to the hospital in the morning. I was up before the sun, ready to go. When my aunt came to get me, she began to explain that my mom had a few issues during the surgery that the doctors didn't expect but that she was going to be just fine. I couldn't wait to go see her.

After a brief ride to the hospital, we were on the elevator headed up to the 2nd floor to ICU (Intensive

Care Unit). Upon entering her room, the first thing I saw was a big machine going up and down next to her bed. It was explained to me, "this machine is breathing for your mom." It made me extremely sad to see her in this condition; laying still in a hospital bed not being able to communicate with me. We kept our visit short so that she could get some rest.

I struggled to get that image out of my head. Days would go by and she would finally begin showing signs of improvement. Before long, she was able to finally come home and finish her recovery. I was so relieved to have her home; it just wasn't the same without her there with us.

The doctors were so surprised with how well she recovered considering all she had been through. We were shocked with how much weight she was losing. She ended up losing over 100 pounds and looked and felt great. So much so that she was released by her doctor to return to work. Her job was at a local dry cleaner in Millville, New Jersey, just about 15 minutes from our home. She loved her job and she worked so hard so that we could have a good life.

Shortly after returning back to work, she tripped over a rug that had a corner piece flipped over. That day was the start of her life as a disabled, single, mother of three. After the fall, she went to the hospital with stomach pain near her incision site. While there, the doctors would discover that she had torn open the incision from her surgery from the inside. It would need to be repaired immediately. This would be a high-risk surgery for her considering everything she had endured with the initial procedure.

They were able to successfully repair the damage, but it would be the beginning of a long list of surgeries that she would need all because of the fall she took at work. In the coming months and years, she would suffer from infections so bad she would have to be hospitalized for days. Eventually, a mesh would also need to be put in to hold together the portion of stomach she had left.

You can imagine how difficult it was for not only her but for us kids as well. Trying to properly recover surgery after surgery and make sure we were taken care of at the same time was a big task. Again, she made it happen with the support of family and close friends. This may have forced us to "grow up" a bit quicker as we would have to pitch in but we remained thankful that she was here with us and would do whatever we had to do to pull through this as a family.

Years and years of surgeries and hard times left my mom disabled and stole her best years away from her. There were many restrictions and a lot of the things she once enjoyed were just not possible in this moment. She would never be able to return to work nor would she ever return to the way of life she had before the surgery. Through it all, she felt blessed to still be alive.

A Medical Mishap

A young boy with a lot going on in his personal life. The smile hides the worry that lived inside his body during this challenging time for his family

Chapter 4

A SAVING GRACE

My home environment came with its own societal stigmas. As a young boy I didn't let that bother me. You see it didn't matter to me where I lived, where I slept at night or if people made fun of me for the small trailer I called home. What was important to me and stands out from my childhood was all the fun memories that came with living in a "close knit" environment even if that environment was a trailer park.

For me, living in a trailer park growing up was fun and exciting. You always had friends to play with. No matter what day of the week it was or the time of day, there was always someone outside to hang out with. I became more like family to a few friends I met while living there. Their parents pretty much became my "adopted family." We would take turns sleeping over each other's houses and they would take me along with them on trips.

One certain group of us became very close. Matt, Vincent, George, Corey and Curtis were pretty much who I hung out with the most. I loved playing sandlot football or baseball out in the big field behind my trailer. It was usually where we would spend most of our time.

Almost every Wednesday night, a van from Bridgeton Assembly of God Church, would pull up with a man we all knew in the driver's seat. Mr. Elmer lived in the same trailer park we did. He always made sure to invite us to church every week. Every time he came around, a bunch of kids would jump in the van and I would just deny the invite and walk home. My family didn't go to church and I wasn't sure it was a place for me.

Mr. Elmer would continue to ask me week after week. After discovering that two of my closest friends went to the same church, I finally decided to give it a try. When I first arrived, they sent me to Royal Rangers, kind of like Boy Scouts. I wasn't quite old enough to attend the youth group at the church, therefore this program was where I would spend my time on Wednesday nights.

This experience was so different from anything that I had ever been a part of. Even though I didn't think I was really good at it, I can remember the Commanders trying to encourage me week after week to keep coming out. They made me feel like I belonged there. I ended up staying for about a year until I was old enough to move up to the youth group.

Wow, what a difference it was for me. My first night in youth group was something that I have never forgotten to this day. It was called the 79er's club. We would meet on Wednesday nights from 7:00pm–9:00pm. To my surprise, Mr. Elmer from the church van was also the youth leader.

At this point, I had made some friends from Royal Rangers that started coming to youth group with me. Every time Mr. Elmer would try to teach, we would do something to interrupt him. Well it didn't take long for him to teach me a lesson. One night, in the middle of youth group, he asked me to stand up and walk over to the far-right side of the room to a blue chair. Soon after I got to the chair, he told me to kneel down and put my face down until the end of the night. I was so embarrassed; I couldn't believe this was happening to me.

That had to be one of the longest nights of my life. After service, Mr. Elmer approached me and told me not to get in the van, he was going to take me home. I was definitely not looking forward to that ride home however, I have to say, that ride home changed my life forever. He began to ask me questions and engage in a conversation where he would explain to me that he knew all of this was new to me. He went on to assure me that I wouldn't be asked to not come back. He explained, "this is exactly what you need; tough love never hurt anyone."

Mr. Elmer took me to Burger King that night. Definitely not what I expected to happen. As we sat and ate, he continued to talk to me about how the only thing perfect in the world was God himself. I was blown away by how he was treating me even though

I acted up during the service. From that night on, Mr. Elmer and myself would develop a wonderful friendship. This was the beginning of what would continue to change my life forever.

After the life changing conversation with Mr. Elmer, I knew I belonged at Bridgeton Assembly of God. I would continue to get on and off of that van every Wednesday night like clockwork. Little did I know that more than just the relationships that I was forming with people, the most important relationship in my life was developing as well. That was my relationship with God! Without the opportunities given to me by simply taking the chance and hopping in that van, I don't know what roads in life I would have traveled down. What I do know is that I'm glad I don't have to look back at what that life may have brought me.

Mr. Elmer with my friend Eric, both relationships that were possible because I decided to get in that van.

Chapter 5

MEETING THE MENTORS

Life was always crazy at 110 Tips Trailer Park. There wasn't a day that went by when something crazy didn't take place. My older brother Brian seemed to find a way to make every day interesting. Being 6 years older than me, he was into things that weren't always good or right. Only having one brother and no father figure, he was really all I had to look up to. Brian was really big into hanging in the streets and getting into trouble. It wasn't really all his fault at first. Being raised by a single mom on disability, it wasn't easy to have enough money to pay the bills, let alone have any extra to hand out to us kids.

My brother turned to selling drugs to help make ends meet for the house and my mom. I'm sure my mom didn't always know the extent of what was going on right under her nose. My brother was the man of the house and I wanted to be just like him at one time. That didn't last long as he would find himself in and out of jail; not a lifestyle that interested me. I have to say that it actually encouraged me to stay on the right track honestly.

While attending church, I had the opportunity to meet a lot of people who treated me like family, like I belonged there. I got to experience a whole new meaning to the word "family." At the young age of 11, I was able to meet the owner of a local pizza shop in my town, Mr. Reds. He was a Deacon at the Bridgeton Assembly of God Church. This guy always had a smile on his face. He ended up being my Sunday school teacher for some time. During my time in his Sunday school class, I would always ask him for a job. His response would remain the same, "in due time. Your time will come soon enough."

Reds, the guy who always wore a welcoming smile.

I just loved being around Mr. Reds. He and his wife, Mrs. Scott, would invite a bunch of us kids over after church to hang out and have lunch. They treated us like their own children, of which they had two, a son and a daughter. The house was so big, much different than the trailer in which I lived. We loved Summers at the Scott house. They had a huge in-ground pool. And speaking of pool, Mr. Reds had a pool table in the basement. He would always play us in a game of pool when time allowed. He was the best pool player I had ever seen. The best memories were when he would show us his "trick" shots. None of us ever wanted to leave when the time came. These two were definitely one of a kind!

You know the old saying "be careful what you wish for?" well that couldn't have been any truer. Early one Saturday morning I heard a knock at the door. I was actually sleeping over a friend's house and was called down to get the door. To my surprise there stood Mr. Reds. As I opened the door, he said "it's your turn, you ready to work?" I began to explain to him that it wasn't the best timing as I had plans to go to the shore with my friend and his parents for the day. I was hoping he would be okay and tell me to start on a different day; unfortunately, that was not the case. He went on to explain that he didn't know the next time he would need me. I was honestly struggling in my head however, what he said next changed the game for me. He asked, "are you getting paid to go to the shore today?" Before I could respond he told me that he would wait out in the van for a few minutes, the choice was mine to make. There was no way I could pass up on this offer.

I flew upstairs, changed my clothes, said my goodbyes and out the door I ran. I couldn't believe my chance had finally come. This opportunity would help me and my family so much. Who would have known this would just be the beginning of one of the strongest relationships I'd ever build?

Things were changing so rapidly for me. Soon after beginning the 79er's club with Mr. Elmer, our church decided to look for a full time Youth Pastor which would mean the end of the 79er's club. This caused a lot of the youth to stop coming including myself. One day, while at home with my mom, there was a knock at the door. To my surprise, I heard some people talking and asking if I was home. My mom called me out to meet our guest. In my living room stood a few of the youth leaders and the new Youth Pastor. They were taking him around to meet all of the kids that had been attending the 79er's club. I was a little nervous, but he seemed pretty cool after chatting with him for a little bit. Before they left, they invited me to come check out the new youth group that coming Wednesday night.

Left, Mr. Elmer and Right, Pastor Fabian. I'm pretty sure they were thinking "What are we going to do with that Robbie Johnson kid?"

The day finally arrived, it was Wednesday and time for youth group. After arriving at the church, we were greeted by our new Youth Pastor, Fabian Kalapuch and his wife Dawn. Turns out, they were so nice and fun to be around. It was definitely different, but a good different. As time went on, my relationship with Pastor Fabian grew. He had become more than a Youth Pastor to me, he was more like a father figure that I was so desperately looking for. He not only worried about teaching me about God, but also cared about me as a person. Mr. Reds and Pastor Fabian's influence on my life continued to change me in the direction I so gravely needed. They came alongside my mom and helped her anyway they could to make sure me and my family were taken care of. Those two were so extremely influential to me however, by no means were they the only ones who had an impact on me. So many men in the church had taken the role of an uncle, big brother, father and so many other roles in my life as I grew. I will never forget all those who took the time out of their lives to pour into mine. The saying, "it takes a village", could not be any truer about my life as a whole.

Chapter 6

BROKEN HOME

I think we all have an idea growing up what a perfect home is supposed to look like. Unfortunately, we have to do what we have to do when it comes to how we grow up. Nobody ever says, "I want to be a part of a broken home." I may just be the exception to that rule. I would love to say everything growing up was perfect; but is that even such a thing? We were pretty much the definition of lower class. My mom tried her best to provide for us.

For most of my childhood, my mom had a live-in boyfriend. While she was still able to work, she was the one who went to work while her boyfriend Eddie, stayed home and looked after the house. He was the one who made sure I got on the bus in the morning and got off in the afternoon. Along with making some of the meals and doing laundry he was also the one cleaning the house. That was all good and appreciated however, it didn't help pay the bills. This became an even bigger financial problem after my mom was unable to return to work.

So here we are, me, my mom, Eddie, my brother and sister all living in a two-bedroom trailer. Again, I was mainly confined to the living room couch or floor to sleep. Eddie loved to drink. He would drink from the time he woke up til the time he went to bed. My sister Tonia never saw eye to eye with Eddie. Fights would break out more times than I would like to admit. Tonia would try to fix things, but my mom would stick up for Eddie and things wouldn't change.

My brother Brian liked to go out and drink as well. He was a pretty mean drunk. Talk about an explosion, get Brian and Eddie together after they had both been drinking. Many nights I would pray that someone would ask me to stay at their house. Brian also sold drugs to help my mom pay the bills and keep her head above water. There would be times when I would come home, and my brother would be at the dining room table bagging up dope while my mom was making dinner. I don't think my mom ever thought what he was doing was good but understood it needed to happen for us to survive.

As a child, I saw more than I'd like to admit. I had many times where I would find myself in the middle of a bunch of craziness that comes with people who drink, and have drugs being sold out of the house. The whole drug thing brought on many problems of their own. Our trailer was broken into many times with people trying to find drug proceeds or the drugs themselves. The Police were very familiar with Brian. Many times, the Police would ride up to our house with their guns drawn trying to find Brian and the drugs.

On two separate occasions, my mom and I were home alone when the local task force busted in with active warrants to search our house. They put my mom and myself in handcuffs until the raids were complete. My brother was never around when the raids happened. During one of the raids, they actually arrested my mom and took her to the jailhouse until my brother turned himself in. They allowed me to be released to family because of my age.

During this time, Tonia had relocated to the West Coast to better her future, so she wasn't around for the aftermath. Sooner rather than later, Brian was sentenced to up to 5 years in prison for his drug involvement. My mom was still suffering from medical issues, so Tonia decided to move back to help us out. When she arrived, Eddie was asked to leave immediately. With Brian in prison and Eddie out of the house, things actually took a turn for the worse before they got better.

Eventually, we found a new normal. Between my mom finally getting her state disability and my sister working, bills were getting paid. I tried to help out too with whatever money I would get from doing small jobs. Many would say that we were "the black sheep" of the family. Regardless of what anyone thought, or how bad it got, or what we had to endure, we always stuck together. Many of us have things we go through during our childhood; the difference is how we grow from these experiences to help us be better human beings.

Chapter 7

BEYOND BLOOD

I was very blessed to have so many people play a part of my childhood and teenage years. I don't know where I would have ended up if those special people didn't step up and take on those roles. During my teenage years, I was pretty big into church at Bridgeton Assembly of God. No one from my family attended church there. When I began, I was a "van kid." Leaders of the church would drive around and pick you up on Wednesday nights and Sunday mornings for services. For me though, the van rides didn't last long.

I started catching rides with different families throughout the church that would offer to pick me up and drop me back off afterwards. I had never experienced that type of love from people who were not related to me before. I can remember our phone ringing most Sunday mornings; Mr. Phil would call and make sure I was up and getting ready. He always made sure I was there if I wanted to be there. Everybody at church made me feel like I was a part of their family. Oftentimes, I would even go home with a different family on Sunday and spend time with them. It was so cool to have people who loved me and took care of me regardless of my circumstances.

Through my time at Bridgeton Assembly of God, I got to meet a lot of wonderful people. Some of those same people are still close to me 30 years later. My closest friendship to this day is a kid I met in youth group. Shelton had a pretty similar story to my own. He was raised by a single mother; however, he was an only child. He also had a pretty hard life growing up. We hit it off pretty much right away. We both liked to clown around and make fun all the time. Like myself, Shelton attended church alone without his family. I'm pretty sure he was one of those "van kids" for a while as well.

Before you knew it, Shelton and I were inseparable. They actually used to call us the "bopsie twins". Shelton had a job at Big John's Pizza. Remember that Sunday school teacher Mr. Reds who owned a local pizza shop? Well that is where Shelton worked, the place I had continually asked for an opportunity to work at. Turns out, I eventually got my opportunity however it was rare that the two of us worked together.

Shelton soon became a part of my family. My mom considered him as a son as did his mom, Ms. Shirley, consider me as her son. God knew what He was doing when he allowed our paths to cross. Just about 28 years later and we are still the best of friends, actually we are more than friends, we are brothers. Shelton is a very successful government employee with a wife and two daughters, my beautiful nieces. Even though we are separated by about 2 and a half hours of traveling distance, we would both run to each other's rescue if the need should ever arise.

Shelton, my wife, Heather and myself at my 40th birthday party. On this night, Heather asked him to do the toast, let's just say there wasn't a dry eye in the place. He is more than my best friend; he is my brother.

Our Youth Pastor, Fabian, had a very large impact on my life as well. When he arrived at our church, he was very young and newly married to his wife Dawn. They had just graduated from Zion Bible Institute in Rhode Island. Pretty much everything was a work in progress. I'm sure they didn't know much themselves about life but that didn't stop them from coming right in and connecting with us from day one.

Pastor Fabian was all about building relationships and showing us all about God's love. I'm confident that from the very beginning, this was no easy job for him. He was given a broken youth group that needed some restructuring and guidance. Together with his wife, they managed to put their own spin on it and turned it into what would be some of the best times of my life. We learned so much from them during our days in the youth group. He taught us that we needed to love ourselves just as much as we needed to love God.

This guy would come up with some of the craziest things to do with us. When it was time to learn, he would get serious and teach his heart out. Watch out though when it was time to let loose and chill. Although he had a job to do, he also went above and beyond to make sure I stayed on the right path. He developed a very good relationship with my mom as well. When there were problems at my house, Pastor Fabian and Dawn would allow me to stay with them. I spent quite a bit of time with them and they always made sure I was taken care of. The two of them definitely had a huge impact on my life and taught me just what a family should be.

Between Reds, my mentor, and Pastor Fabian, I know that I wouldn't be who I have become without their love and support throughout my adolescent and teenage years. As Reds expressed to me before his passing. "I'm glad I didn't waste my time on you!" I will be forever grateful for the time they invested in me and my future.

Even though these two men had the largest impact, there were so many others who played a part as well. Throughout the years, you may be told things that you might not understand at the time, but trust me, later in life you will appreciate all those who took the time to invest in you becoming a better YOU!!

Chapter 8

SAVED

At one time, I thought just the fact that I went to church was enough. Enough for what? Well I'm not quite sure I fully understood the spiritual principle behind attending church. During my time in youth group, I would hear all about how much God loved me and that He sent His Son to die on the cross so I could have eternal life. Being young and doing what most young people do, I barely listened to what was being said. My reasons for going to church were to hang out with friends and get away from all the craziness of my home life.

Being a part of the youth group allowed me to meet different kids from all around the city and surrounding areas. Some I got to know better than others. A few of them became more like family than friends. Youth group laid the foundation for my walk with Christ and who I am today. It was so much more than just a church service. It was a huge family that loved unconditionally.

One of our many fun filled Youth Group events with the group of teenagers who became my extended family.

I was able to serve on the Youth Group Council as President for a few years. This would allow me to work closely with Pastor Fabian on upcoming events throughout the year. I really liked being able to be a part of something. The position gave me purpose. The Youth Council was a small group of people who served as a board to help lead the direction of our youth group.

Another area I loved to be a part of was our band. Our worship band needed a drummer. I never played an instrument in my life, but I didn't let that stop me. I wasn't quite sure where to start. Pastor Fabian connected me with our church worship team drummer, Mr. Mark. I began taking lessons to help me become a better drummer. Living in a trailer didn't make it an easy task for me to be a drummer. The only place I could practice was at the church or on my practice pad. Even though it didn't come natural, I continued to press forward and do the best I could. After all the uncertainties, our youth worship ended up being pretty good. I still think they were just being nice to me all those years. Regardless, I wouldn't trade those experiences.

While my time in youth group was amazing, there is one Wednesday night in particular that truly changed my life. The night started off as usual; we played a few songs, took offering, then came the message. Pastor Fabian told us all about how God made us in His image. in his image. We were built for greatness. He told us that the devil comes to lie, steal and destroy our lives. However, God sent His only Son to die for us so we could have the opportunity to live in freedom, saved by His Grace. As he continued to talk, I began to weep. I was in a place in my life where I didn't know how I could face another day. I felt like this message was just for me. There had to be over thirty other kids in the room. There I sat at just 16 years old broken, looking for something new. I knew how I was living wasn't working.

Toward the end of his message, Pastor Fabian gave an alter call for anyone who wanted to give their life to Jesus. I couldn't hold back any longer, there was a fire inside of me and I made my way to the alter to receive the best gift ever, eternal life. I received a fresh start that very night.

Chapter 9

FLUNKED OUT

As a small child, I loved school. I attended Fairfield Primary School then Fairfield Middle School before ending my days at Cumberland Regional High School. During my Elementary School days, I was such a good student and was a very fast learner. My relationships with my teachers were awesome. You know those kids, the "teacher's pet" well that was me. Mr. Devono was my 4th grade teacher and my favorite by far. He would always show us magic tricks and tell us that we could do anything we put our mind to.

Later on, in Middle School, the work got a little harder and friendships started to get a little more complicated. Not to mention, my mom's health began deteriorating during my early Middle School days. Things at home were not always easy to handle either. Once I had reached 7th grade, we had to start changing classes throughout the school day. Not really an easy transition for a kid that was used to spending the whole day in one classroom. I really had no choice but to adjust to the new norm. Before long, I was doing what was expected and enjoying myself at the same time. Middle School wasn't that bad after all.

Now High School, well that was a whole different ball game. From the very first day of my Freshman year, it just didn't seem right for me. The building was so much bigger than the Middle School. Because it was a Regional High School, it was filled with kids from all the surrounding towns. Friends I had made in Middle School were spread out, so it made it hard to keep those connections as we did not share very many classes together if any. It was like starting all over again, something I was not looking forward to.

I began missing school, so I didn't have to face being in a new school and all the challenges that came with it. My mom was sick and in and out of the hospital a lot during my Freshman year. That made it pretty easy for me to stay home basically whenever I wanted. My sister would be the one who would enforce that I go to school. I used to go as far as getting up and getting dressed just to pretend to walk to the bus stop. I would then find a place to hide until my sister would leave for work. I can remember climbing up on my neighbor's boat and laying across the back seat and falling back to sleep. Not my finest moments, but I'm being honest.

I did whatever I could not to go to school. Out of the 180-day school year, I missed over 90 days of my Freshmen year. Again, not my smartest decision. I pretty much screwed myself from ever being able to graduate with my class on time. After realizing just how bad my situation had become the following year, I had to really buckle down and get serious about what I needed to do to "make up for lost time."

I was evaluated by our school child study team, and after further consideration, they came to the conclusion that with my mom being sick, my home life not being the best, that my best interest would be for them to see me on a weekly basis to help keep me on track. In case you were wondering, it was frowned upon by my peers to be a high schooler who was being seen by the child study team. However, the experience for me was actually not that bad. The staff were amazing, and they worked very hard to see to it that I was reaching my potential. They definitely had my back during the times that became tough for me. During my Sophomore and Junior years, I had to work extra hard to make up for my wasted Freshmen year. I really tried hard to get my act together.

Early on in my Senior year, it was realized that I was still going to come up short with credits in order to graduate with my class. The child study team awarded me credits for working and attending church. They honestly did everything they could possibly do to get me to the finish line. After realizing that no matter what I did, I would still be short the graduation credit requirement, my Mentor Reds Scott and another close friend at the time told me about this program that the State offered.

Apparently, I just had to register to take the High School Proficiency test in Atlantic City, New Jersey and if I passed, I would receive my High School diploma.

That was great news for me! I followed their lead and made an appointment to go take the test. It was only administered on Friday's and you had to take the test in 2 half day portions. With all the disappointment that came with not finishing High School the traditional way, I am proud to say that I didn't give up on that chapter in my life, I passed the exam with 91% and ended up with my diploma before the rest of my graduating class of 1997. There is no doubt in my mind that if I could do it all over again, I definitely would do it the traditional way. However, I know God doesn't make mistakes and His plans are better than ours. Please stay in school and set goals for yourself. You can do anything you set out to do. Some of us like to work harder and go a different route. Regardless of how you get there, just get there! Work smarter, not harder!

High School was my most challenging years with so much going on in my family life. It's the one part of my life I would redo given the chance.

Chapter 10

FULL TIME

So now what? High school was done, and I had no clue what I wanted for my life. It took everything I had just to get my diploma, and College didn't seem too interesting to me. Shortly after getting my diploma my mom, who is disabled got a phone call that she was accepted into a housing program in our area for disabled senior citizens. The unfortunate part was she had to go alone. She could not bring me or my brother with her. I was just 17 at the time and it turned my world upside down. I was working every day to make money just so I could survive.

Fortunately for me the Webster Family who lived close by on Sunset Avenue just across from the trailer park, kindly agreed to let me stay in their basement until I could get my own place. I paid Mrs. Webster $75 a week for a place to lay my head. My own family didn't offer me a place to stay but I never really let that bother me. All that did was give me more ambition and drive to make it on my own. I knew I couldn't do it by just working one job, so the search was on.

Working full-time at Big John's Pizza already I decided to apply at a local video store for some part-time work. Before long I was called to interview for them and they hired me on the spot. Every single dollar I made barely kept the bills paid. I didn't stop there though I always wanted to better myself. I would try job after job to see what paid better and what I wanted to do long-term. Regardless of if I left the pizza shop or not, I knew I always had a spot when I wanted it. I tried so many jobs, mostly part-time while still working at the pizza shop at some capacity. I honestly don't know if there was a job I didn't try. From pizza to banking and from there to meter reading, factory jobs and tons of retail. I even spent a day training for door-to-door marketing. When you have no one to help you or offer financial assistance, you really don't have a choice. No matter what, I had to work if I was going to make it in this world.

One thing that always made me feel good was pizza. My mentor was so great when it came to me trying new things. He always said, "you'll never know unless you try." Regardless of how hard-headed I was, he never gave up on me. He would always tell me to work hard no matter what and it will come.

The original Big John's Pizza in Bridgeton, where it all started for me. This shop is still a famous spot for pizza.

After every job I tried nothing made me feel at home like the pizza shop. Eventually, I quit going from job to job and buckled down at the pizza shop. Reds saw that I was finally growing up, so he decided to allow me to run a few shifts in his stores. At the time he owned three different locations. The main store was in Bridgeton. His second location was on Delsea Drive in Vineland. Glassboro Big John's was the last of the three locations. I was interested in handling shift operations in all three locations. Now that I was able to do more than just cook, it became a little more interesting to me. The more I listened to my boss, the more I learned.

It was so cool only being 18 years old and helping my boss run his three locations. Sometimes it got annoying because I would be the one who would be sent to fix problems that would arise. The only down-fall was that I was always at work when everybody else was off. You have to work nights and weekends in the pizza world. I wouldn't change the time I spent alongside my boss / mentor. I gained so much business sense just seeing him take care of daily operations.

I remember learning that when you're in school, you wish you were out in the real word. Then, once you are actually out in the real world you wish you were back in school and living at home. Hard work definitely pays off. After living in my friend's basement for a few months, I was able to save up enough money to rent my first one-bedroom apartment. It was such an accomplishment for me. Just before I moved in, my car which I was making payments on decided to have mechanical issues. It ended up having a bad timing belt and a few other issues that added up quickly. Too many things were happening at once; I had a car pay-ment, full coverage insurance, $75 a week for rent, and an opportunity to move into my own apartment with a broken-down car. I had big boy problems and didn't know which way to go.

After days of thinking about what to do I had to voluntarily give my car back. I couldn't find anyone to help me out by lending me the money so at the moment, an apartment was my priority. I had no clue what the repercussions would later be with the car but at the time I had to do what was best for me. From the age of 17 to 18 years old, my life was changing at

a rapid pace. From working full-time, failed relationships, a new apartment and trying to figure out life
in general, well let's just say growing up isn't easy!

Chapter 11

TRUE LOVE

Dating? With everything that was going on, that was the last thing on my mind. I had recently gotten out of a relationship with a girl that had lasted a few years. During that relationship, so much of my life was changing. You think you're going to be with your high-school sweetheart forever. Most likely that will turn out to be false, for me at least it did. Once that was over, it was time for me to just chill out and focus on taking care of me. Sounded good at the time at least.

I was working like crazy. Some weeks two or three jobs. Just trying to stay busy and figure out what was next for me was enough. I had learned that Janie, my birth mother, had passed away. At the time it didn't affect me since she was never really a part of my life. Looking back, I have no regrets. As I have gotten older, I sometimes think what life would be like if she were still around. Would we have ever reconnected? It doesn't matter now, like the saying goes, "God works all things together for my good!" He knew what He was doing.

I eventually joined our local crime watch organization to occupy some of my idle time. It was there that I met a few friends that ran the concession stands during the Invitational Baseball Tournament in Bridgeton at the city park. The Invitationals ran for 2 weeks in August at night. I was asked to help out in the concession stands for a few nights due to a shortage on help. It was right up my alley; foodservice was my thing.

They asked me to work at the candy and snow cone section of the stand. "That should be fun" I thought to myself. There I was making perfect snow cones for the crowd in no time. It was actually a lot more fun than I originally thought it would be. Throughout the night the ball boys would stop by the stand and ask for a free snow cone. Me, having the soft heart I have, I started hooking them up. I watched those boys run after foul balls all night. The least I could do was cool them off with a snow cone.

Towards the end of the second night of me being there, here walked up this cute, strawberry blondish girl who really made me take a second look at her. She began to ask where her brother kept getting all the snow cones and candy from. At first, I wanted to lie to her, but I ended up coming clean and telling her it was all me. I was blown away by how beautiful this girl was. I kept rambling on, so she didn't leave the stand. It was time for me to turn up the charm. From the very first minute I saw her I knew this chick was different. Something about her was special. Eventually she ended up walking away and thanking me for taking care of her little brother.

Now here I am, not long out of a relationship, which I had told myself not to even think about another one for quite some time and then she shows up. Just something about this girl, I couldn't get out of my head. As I was leaving that night from the stand, I offered to come back the next night with hopes to run into her again. The home team weren't the only ones hitting a homerun that next night.

I showed up to my post, set up shop and here comes my little ball boy again. The whole time I'm talking to him I'm looking out at the crowd in hopes of seeing his sister. The whole night goes by and no signs of the beauty queen. Just my luck, I figured it was too good to be true. After cleaning up and saying goodbye to everyone I began to walk towards my car. When at last I see who I've been looking for all night. I couldn't help but to walk up and say hi.

After talking for a short time, I realized they were stranded at the field. Her parents were late to come back to pick them up. So, me, being the nice guy, offered to take them home. To my surprise she accepted and off we went. Conversation started off pretty slow. I just wanted to get to know her better. I couldn't shake this feeling that she left me with, it was like nothing I've ever felt. Before she got out of the car, we exchanged numbers. I couldn't wait to get home and call her. I ended up working that stand almost every night, so I had an excuse to see her.

Before long, our phone conversations would last through the night. Some nights we would even fall asleep together on the phone. It didn't take long before we started dating. I knew from the minute I laid eyes on her she was the one. I'll never forget that night, August 26, 1998 was the night that Heather Borgese and I started dating. It was the start of a new me!

Heather and I as a young and head over heels in love couple.

She gave me purpose. I looked forward to getting off work so we could spend time together. I never wanted our time together to end. Heather was a little younger than me. I was already out of school; she was in her junior year of high school. It didn't seem to bother her parents though. I'm not quite sure if they knew the age difference at the time. Heather was so mature and focused in life. Even with her still being in high school, she was different than any other girl I knew. We became inseparable in such a short amount of time. We did everything together.

Her parents allowed me to come and hang out with the family at her house. Her friends became my friends and my friends became hers. I was even allowed to vacation with her family in Disney in May of 1999. Her mom and dad were so cool. Heather had two little brothers Joey and Justin. Those boys were always around us. They couldn't wait to tell her parents whatever they could to get us in trouble. I guess that's what little brothers are for. With me being the baby of my family, I never got to experience what having younger siblings was like.

Heather with her mom Gladys and two brothers Joey and Justin.

I wish I could say our whole relationship was perfect but that would totally be a lie. Just like anything else we had to work through our differences and grow together if we wanted what we had to last especially since we were both pretty young. Most people didn't think we were going to last. One of the most challenging times for us, especially Heather, was during her parents' divorce. It's never easy to watch your family being torn apart. It broke my heart to watch Heather be pulled apart during this unsettling time for her family. She felt she needed to be the mom to her brother's, companion to her dad and try her best to be a part of our relationship too. Divorce is never easy, and Heather took it very hard.

Heather with her dad Joe, and brothers Joey and Justin. Family has always been important to her.

Her life as she knew it literally fell apart. All I knew at the time was that no matter what I would be there for her. It actually made her grow up a lot faster than she would probably like to admit. I stood by her side through all of it. I know she would do the same for me. We had spent just about 2 years dating at this point and there was no doubt in my mind that she was my one true love. I needed to make her my wife.

January 31, 2001 is a day I will never forget. I asked the love of my life to be my wife. I was at the pizza shop on a Tuesday afternoon working the morning shift. Not long after the lunch crowd had slowed down, I was making boxes on the front counter and looked up at the TV. To my surprise the show was asking if anyone would like to be a part of their surprise proposal Valentine's Day show. I had remembered Heather always telling me if and when I ever propose that she wanted it to be in front of a lot of people. What better than National TV? I wrote the number down and finished my shift. After deciding exactly how I wanted to do this, I couldn't come up with a better way than on the TV show. I decided to give it a shot. They took my information and told me I would be hearing from a producer soon.

Within a couple of days that phone call came, I was more nervous than ever before. I wanted to make this happen so bad. The process for them to get to know you is crazy. I think I talked to their Producer's just about every day. They wanted to make sure they found the best fit for the show. During the process they needed to speak to Heather. They told me to play along with the idea of it being for a chance to win a trip to Hawaii. They told Heather the show was a couple's compatibility contest. After the interview process was complete, they told us they would be making their final picks for the show in the coming days. We were told they would call either way regardless if we made it or not.

Heather would make me answer all kinds of questions about her, she would constantly drill me. The questions would range from what her favorite food was to where she was born to her favorite color and so on. Boy talk about being annoyed. This was all taking place before we even found out if we would make the show or not. Finally, the call came. They wanted to make sure we were both on the phone before they told us. The producer starts off by saying how close the contest was. They told us over 800 couples applied for the show. The time had come, we were so nervous and excited at the same time. She paused then began congratulating us on making the show. "You have to be kidding me this cannot be happening to us." Don't forget the whole time Heather thought the show was for a trip to Hawaii.

We were told the show was being taped in just over a week from the day we got the call. I was freaking out I had so much to do and time was flying by. That following week was nuts for me. Between Heather making me answer every question about her under the sun and her learning about me, I was exhausted. Producers of the show needed to talk with me alone to setup the perfect way to pop the question. After a few days of talking back and forth they asked me what Heather's favorite game show was. At the time "Who Wants to Be A Millionaire" was very popular. Heather would try her best to answer all the questions correctly every time we watched it. They thought a spin-off of that show would be perfect.

Before we knew it, a long white limo pulled up outside my house to pick us up and take us to New York City for the show. It was actually the night before they tape the show. The limo dropped us off at the Excelsior Hotel on 81st Street in Manhattan. We were left a welcome package at the front desk with instructions for the next morning. Here we are two kids from little old Bridgeton, New Jersey about to embark on the Big Apple at night.

Myself in the limo heading to the Big Apple.

Heather all ready for a trip to the Big Apple for the biggest surprise of her life.

We had no idea where to go. I just wanted to see as much as I could. We decided to walk around after midnight in the middle of the city. Unfortunately, it didn't take long for us to realize we had no clue what or where we would be going. Back to the hotel it was. Speaking of hotel, our room wasn't much bigger than my bathroom in my house. It blew my mind all that they fit in that little tiny room. Honestly it didn't really matter, we just needed somewhere to sleep for the night. Out of nowhere, Heather jumps up and runs into the bathroom. "No!" I couldn't believe it; tell me she is not in there getting sick? Of all the days and times to catch the bug, really the day we were about to tape the show?

She was able to take some medicine and get herself together enough to leave the hotel on time. I couldn't sleep all night because of how bad my nerves were. I also needed to make sure she didn't see the ring I was hiding. What a rush, driving in a New York taxi on our way to the set of the show. I was thinking to myself, if Heather doesn't get sick in here, we'll be just fine for the show. Shortly after arriving they split us up. We wouldn't see each other again until showtime.

To my surprise, we were picked to open the show. Talk about being nervous, I have no idea how I went through with it all. I had invited a few of Heather's family to be a part of our special day. Heather had no clue what was about to take place. The show starts, I'm already on-stage sitting waiting for my introduction. The theme music starts and out comes Queen Latifah. Yep, we made it on the Queen Latifah talk show that aired on Fox 29. After asking me about how we met and what made me want to marry her, Heather was asked to come on out. Remember she has no idea what is about to happen.

Queen Latifah explains we are going to play a spin-off of "Who Wants to Be A Millionaire" to see if we will win that awesome trip to Hawaii. First question was "What is the name of the bar where everybody knows your name?" Before I could even look at Heather, she shouts out "Cheers!" The audience applauds and she gets all happy. Second question, "What was the name of the movie about a woman's softball team featuring Madonna?" Again, without even asking me, Heather shouts out "A League of Their Own." Queen Latifah shouts "You're right again!"

The time had finally come for the third and final question for a grand prize trip to Hawaii; or at least that's what she thought, but it wasn't that easy. "How many times has Tiger Woods appeared on the cover of Sports Illustrated?" Queen Latifah asked us. Heather and I looked at each other knowing darn well we had no idea. I asked to use our one and only "Latifah Lifeline." I said, "let's ask Heather's dad." She immediately nudged me, whispering "he doesn't know that!" She really wanted that trip to Hawaii. The lights came on in the audience with her dad standing next to Queen Latifah. She looked puzzled as her dad began nervously stumbling to introduce himself. I said, "Actually I have a more important question to ask you, I'd like to ask for permission to marry your daughter. I turned and got down on my knee and asked her to be my wife. She was pretty stunned, at first nobody heard her response. Queen Latifah asked, "Was that a yes?" Thank God she said yes. The audience went nuts; we were both kind of overwhelmed, I think. It was one of the best days of my life. Hawaii would have to wait! Queen Latifah surprised us with tons of gifts, a getaway, free flowers and any dress Heather wanted from David's Bridal. From the very first day I saw her I wanted this day to be a reality and now it was.

Chapter 12

ARE YOU MY DADDY?

From a very early age I would often ask who my dad was. Going to school with kids who had a mom and a dad always made me think about my situation. Growing up with a single mom for most of my life made me appreciate her and her tireless efforts to fill the shoes of both a mom and a dad. My mom never made us feel like we were missing anything from our daily lives. On top of being adopted, then raised by a single mother, the question stayed in the back of my mind. I was pretty sure I wasn't hatched out of an egg. The question was who was my dad?

As I got older the more curious, I became. I would always think about asking my mom questions about my adoption and if she knew my birth father, but I never wanted to upset her or make her think I was trying to replace her. Honestly, I just wanted to find out more about my family history. I'm sure you can relate how I felt, not knowing where I came from. Not knowing who your biological parents are and what your heritage is can leave you with so many unknown questions about who you are.

During my teenage years I would say from about 14 years old and up I would hint around to my mom about looking for my dad. One day to my surprise my mom mentioned that she came across my adoption papers and that there was a name of a potential father on there. She then went on to explain how my birth mother would always have a new guy around her all the time. She told me to not get my hopes up but that she was totally fine with me trying to find my birth father. She told me I deserved to find the answers I had been looking for. I knew it wouldn't be easy, but I was so committed after I received the green light from my mom. She had no idea how excited I became.

After reading the adoption papers and discussing the findings with my mom, she said she remembered the name of the guy who signed the papers. My mom went on to tell me she thought he was originally from North Jersey and had worked within the city government in Bridgeton. Not long after getting the documents I started trying to locate my dad. With this all taking place in the late 1990s, I didn't have a lot of resources to help me in my search. The biggest resource I had to use was the 411 option on our local phone service. You could dial in and after getting an operator you could tell them a name and address and receive a phone number for that person. It honestly was such a cool tool to use to find people's numbers.

From about the age of 14 years old I would call 411 and ask for Gary Weltchek. My search would always end up with "no number found." While talking to my mom throughout the years she would tell me things that she recalled about my potential father. I started to tell the operator his name and that he lived in North Jersey. I was just guessing and hoping for the best. One of the craziest parts about the whole process was that every operator would ask me to spell his last name. I would read off my adoption papers the best way that I could. Whoever this guy was he didn't sign so clear and it was hard to understand. This continued for years until I finally just gave up hope.

I was about 19 years old and finally met the love of my life and spent most of my free time with her. While dating and getting to know each other better, Heather would often ask me questions about my life and how my childhood was. We finally began to understand each other and what our past was all about. She would ask from time to time about my search for my dad. With her encouragement I started my search up again. One night while hanging out with Heather, I decided to give the old 411 another try. I knew it wouldn't get me anywhere, but it was worth a shot. To my surprise this operator asked me for the name and city but never asked me for the spelling. Shortly after I gave her the info she came back and said, "please hold for the number."

I was totally shocked and in disbelief. I started fumbling around nervously trying to get a writing utensil to write down this number that I had been searching after for years. The day had finally come. I was so excited but didn't think it would turn out to be much. At this point regardless if this guy was my dad or not, I was hoping he would have some type of information that would help me in my search for the guy who helped create my being.

It took me days to build up enough courage to even call that number. I was so afraid of what could happen. After days of doubting myself with Heather constantly encouraging me, I decided to make that dreaded phone call. The more numbers I pressed, the more I started to sweat. Before I knew it, I was on the other end of a phone call where I had no clue what I was to say.

No one answered my call, but they had an answering machine that picked up, "You have reached Pat and Gary, please leave a message after the tone." I can leave a message. What should I say? My mind was racing. Shortly after the beep I began to tell them who I was and that I just had a few questions that I thought they could help me answer. Boy was I sweating big time during that phone call.

The days just went by and I never heard back from them. During this time cell phones were not really popular. I may have had a beeper, but I left my home phone number on their machine and asked for a call back, but I also told them I would understand if they didn't call me back. To my surprise about a week and a half later I received a call back. I just so happened to be hanging out with Heather at my apartment. The phone rang and Heather answered. I could hear her talking and soon realized that very well could be the guy I called and left a message for. I was super nervous but totally excited at the same time. Finally, my prayers had been answered and hopefully some of my questions would be soon.

When Heather handed me the phone, I began by saying "thank you so much for calling me back" but it wasn't what I expected on the other end of the call. A woman responded that she was Gary's wife Pat, and it was the least she could do. She went on to apologize for taking so long to call back, but they had been on vacation. I didn't mind one bit; I was just so glad they called me back. Not long after we introduced ourselves, she asked me to explain my situation to her. She was very upfront and told me that Gary wasn't really interested in talking but she felt compelled to at least try to hear my story and help any way she could. We talked for a little over an hour. Before we hung up, she promised that wouldn't be the last time we spoke. What more could I ask for?

Over the next couple of months. Pat and I would talk from time to time. One night during my call Gary finally decided to get on the phone and talk to me. What a super nice guy he was. He apologized right away and explained to me the relationship he had with my birth mother. He was raised in North Jersey, went away to college, and after graduating took a full-time position in Bridgeton, New Jersey with the zoning department. He also worked part-time at a local liquor store.

There he would meet my birth mother Janie. They became very good friends and would hang out from time to time. He would eventually be fired from the city job and decide to return to his hometown to start over. In the late part of November 1978, he left Bridgeton and was never to see my birth mother Janie again. The story started to fit the timeline in my head that made me think that this guy could really be my dad.

I had a few conversations with Gary in the following few weeks. Regardless if he turned out to be my dad or not, we started to become friends. Before long, we mutually decided to have our first meet up in Atlantic City, New Jersey. Gary and his wife Pat were staying at the Hilton Hotel & Casino. They asked us to come down for dinner. I was pretty young and didn't really know what to expect. Heather knew all about what was happening from day to day and she would encourage me to keep moving forward and play it out. I came so far, no need to turn back now.

Without knowing what to expect, I asked Heather's dad to come down with us to make it a little easier for me. Heather's dad was happy for me and agreed to do whatever I needed to make this happen. So here we are August of 2001, potentially meeting my dad for the very first time. My nervous stomach made it almost impossible to even stand there and wait. The anticipation was so over-the-top I couldn't sit still. Looking down the hall, here comes this guy wearing a black polo, blue jeans and loafers. Is this the guy? As he got closer and closer Heather leaned over and said, "That is your dad. You look just like him." He walked up with his wife Pat, shook our hands and introduced himself. Off to dinner we go.

The conversation went surprisingly well. His wife looked at us both and said, "well by the looks of it I'd say we have our answer." I knew from the moment he walked up that he was my dad. As the night went on, we both knew we were Father and Son. Our relationship was great from the start. His wife told us that night that after the very first phone call we had, she hung up and told Gary that I was calling to tell him that I was his son. I couldn't believe that after all those years of searching my hard work had paid off.

As time went on our relationship grew stronger and stronger. From the very first time we talked as father and son I made sure that he knew I wanted nothing more than a relationship / friendship with him. I also made sure he knew that I wasn't mad at the fact he signed off for me to be adopted. I told him it was such an unselfish act and that I was grateful that he allowed me to have a better life than he thought he could provide me with. To this day I cherish all the time we spent together. We did our best to make up for lost time.

Chapter 13

MARRIED WITH CHILDREN

One of the coolest and probably craziest things we ever did was get engaged on The Queen Latifah Show. Now came all the planning for the big day. We decided to get married the following June. That gave us almost a year-and-a-half to make it the most perfect day ever. Heather got together with friends and family and just about put the whole day together. I wanted it to be everything she had always dreamt of. I was okay with just about anything she wanted. Being on the show helped us with our flowers for the day of the wedding and Heather received her dress for free as well. This was a huge blessing as we were financing the wedding pretty much on our own.

Before we knew it, June 15, 2002 was upon us. Excited and nervous I knew I was about to marry my best friend. The day was perfect, and the weather cooperated which was nice since we had an outdoor ceremony. All of our friends and family were there. I was blessed to have my dad and his wife join us for our special day. Remember, we had just met about 10 months prior to my wedding day.

My dad Gary and I on my wedding day. It is such a blessing to
me that he was part of such a big day in my life.

We ended up having about 180 people come to
celebrate with us at our reception following the ceremony. During our time taking photos, we were able to
stop by the place where we first met, the Alden Field
where the Invitational baseball tournament was held
in our city park. The whole day of our wedding seemed
to just be a moment in time. Before we knew it, the
night had come to an end. However, our lives as husband and wife were just beginning.

After the ceremony we just had to capture a photo of where it all started.

A conversation with my mentor Reds after he blessed the food for our reception.

As far as our home life, not much had to change. We were already living together in a small 2-bedroom apartment in Bridgeton, New Jersey. I was glad to finally have my long-time best friend share my last name. I vowed to love her no matter what and she also vowed to love me even on my worst of days. Life was good, she was working at a local law office and I was slinging pies at Big John's Pizza. We were both working full-time jobs doing everything we could to survive.

We were enjoying life together and spending all of our time together. As life has it, things wouldn't always be "perfect." Heather would find out that she was pregnant, only to miscarry 12 weeks into the pregnancy. It was rough on both of us and took a toll on her body. The emotional piece of it was the hardest to watch as there was nothing I could do or say to make it better. As we learned over the years, we had to "give it to God" and trust that He knew better than we did.

He sure does hold our future in His hands. That December, the day after Christmas and on my mom's birthday, Heather surprised me by wrapping up "a late Christmas present", a positive pregnancy test. We were going to be parents after all. What an amazing and scary time for us. We were both so excited once we got past the first trimester. We couldn't wait to find out what we were having. I had dreamt about being a dad for a few years.

Once finding out about a baby coming, I had to really think about my future and figure out a way to provide for them both. I started to think about other stuff like health insurance, a structured work schedule and everything else that comes to mind when you're thinking about bringing a child into the world. It was time for me to grow up and try to figure out what I wanted out of life.

Heather was the cutest pregnant person I'd ever seen. As the time got closer to her delivery date, we started to get a little more nervous about the whole parenting thing. I was really excited about decorating the nursery and going out to buy my little girl clothes. Yes, I was about to become the daddy of a sweet baby girl. On September 3, 2003 we welcomed our precious little girl Kyleigh Ciera Johnson into the world.

My dad Gary holding Kyleigh the week we brought her home from the hospital.

Kyleigh dressed up for Easter. Her personality is still just as big.

Chapter 14

LEAP OF FAITH

So much has changed in my life. Not long ago, I was just a young boy trying to survive. Falling in love with my best friend, getting married and now being a dad; it all happened so quickly. Holding that little girl, I knew she was a part of me, words just can't describe how amazing it made me feel. During that moment when she was in my arms, I knew it was up to me to give her the best life possible. It was no longer about me; my focus had to be all about being a better husband and father for my family. I knew it was time to step up and make some changes for the better for all of us. Heather was working as a legal secretary and I was still making pizzas. Don't get it wrong, we were doing everything we had to make it work. I often hear people talk about waiting to have kids until everything is perfect and the time is "right." My answer to that is the time will never be "right." You will always find a reason or excuse why it can't happen. Having Kyleigh made our lives better than ever before.

We were living in a two-bedroom apartment, driving around in used cars, living week-to-week, paycheck-to-paycheck, but to us life was perfect. I knew all growing up that I wanted to own my own pizza shop. I worked myself up the ranks so to speak. Starting out chopping onions and making boxes, I went on to answering phones and cooking. At the age of 16 I started tossing pizzas around from time to time. I love making pizzas, I just always wanted to make more money. Throughout my career and pizza days, I would try other things. It never failed; I would always find myself back at the counter throwing pies. My mentor in the pizza business was always welcoming when I would call him to see if there was a spot for me. Every time I would return, I just felt like there was more out there for me. I had such a desire to own my own shop. I even went as far as writing up my menu, ideas about how I would decorate, and the hours I would be open.

Living week-to-week didn't leave me much hope for becoming an owner. Heather and I would try to save money, it just seemed almost impossible. We did our best despite weeks at a time without even putting away a dollar. We were just blessed to be able to pay our bills and provide for our baby girl. My father-in-law was a corrections officer and told me about an upcoming civil service test. I did not like the idea about being locked up with criminals one bit but honestly thought it would be a great way to provide for Heather and Kyleigh. I woke up one day and decided to take a ride to the county library to look for the application for the civil service test. Surprisingly there were still a few left at the front desk. Usually those applications run out quickly especially in our area. There really weren't many good job opportunities with medical benefits and pensions without having a college degree. While filling out the application, you could pick more than just State Corrections. There was County Sheriff, County Corrections, and local police too. That got me kind of fired up. In the back of my mind I always wanted to be a cop if I couldn't own my own business. I can even remember all the way back to second grade during Black History Month, we had to decorate a shirt for "I have a dream" week and I drew me dressed as a cop. The fact that there was a chance I could become a cop had me totally fired up to take the civil service test.

When filling out the paperwork you were asked to pick three opportunities in the order you would want to be hired. I chose City Police Department, then County Sheriff, and lastly State Corrections. Even after filling out the application I would still dream of my very own pizza shop. I would randomly talk to people about my dream, which most would respond "good luck with that, it takes money and good credit to start a business. Besides that, you're way too young." All those negative thoughts started getting to my head. Every week we would attend church. I would pray all the time for God to show me if it was His will, just show me the way. Over the years where so many things had gone wrong from trying to do life my way, I realized that I needed to rely on God to guide me and make a way.

In the meantime, I took the Civil Service test and passed with an 84. Soon after getting my results, I received an invitation to start the hiring process for State Corrections. I was very hesitant to accept but I knew that this was what was best for my family. Finally, after months of waiting, my time had arrived for the Academy. It was just weeks away. I was trying to work, stay focused, and spend as much quality time with the family as possible.

One day after checking the mail, I noticed an official letter with my name on it. Another invitation, this one being from our local police department. I couldn't believe what I was reading. I responded and started the process. With all this going on, owning my own shop was still in the back of my mind. I was trying so hard to make my dreams come true. I was excited to be offered jobs with corrections and the local police department, don't get me wrong. I was just doing everything I needed to do at the time to put myself in line to be in one of those two positions in law enforcement.

While in limbo with the academy for the state corrections and the opportunity with the local police department I received a phone call from my boss. He asked me if I had time to go out for lunch. Of course, I never turned down a free lunch. He ended up taking me to his daughter's Pizza Shop. I actually had worked there a few times to help her throughout the years. During our time there, he was asking me all about the corrections stuff and how it was going. I told him the academy was just a few weeks away as long as everything stayed the course. "The local police department offered me a position as well" I told him. He was so proud to hear about all the opportunities I was receiving although he knew the passion, I had for the pizza business and he knew I had always dreamed of owning my own store. Just before leaving his daughter's store he told me he knew of a shop for sale. I got all excited! He asked if I had time to look at it, of course I said yes. He looked with a smirk and said, "you're actually standing in it." His daughter no longer wanted her own store. "This is your chance at your dream" he said. "Wow God, is this real?" I couldn't believe what I was hearing. I couldn't wait to get home and tell Heather. I just knew she would be so happy for me.

Well Heather didn't take the news quite as well as I thought she would. She began to remind me that we didn't have the money or credit to even think about owning a business. What was I thinking? She was absolutely right. I decided I just had to go with the law enforcement thing. It's what was best for us, I would just keep telling myself.

After telling a few friends about the opportunity of owning a pizza shop, one close friend offered to help me write a business plan. I quickly took him up on his offer and began the search to find a way to get a loan for the shop. It was definitely a long shot, but I was willing to exhaust every avenue I could. Every bank I would submit an application to would immediately deny my request.

The day finally arrived, my first day at the Academy for Bridgeton Police Department. I decided that I would rather become a cop than a State Corrections Officer. Not exactly what I was hoping for after I found out I had a chance to own my own pizza shop. Unfortunately, I did not have enough of anything to be able to secure a loan for the amount they were asking for the shop.

The police academy was exhausting, we had to be on the pad (concrete landing) at 5:00a.m. for lineup. I attended our local Academy; therefore, I was able to go home every night. Some of the other Academy's required that you stay on property Monday through Friday. Not that it made much difference, by the time I ironed my uniform, shined my shoes, and shaved my face and head, it was time for bed. There was barely enough time to eat dinner.

On Friday nights, Heather and I would attend our Church's coffee house to help out. This one Friday was a little harder to go. I was kind of mad at God. Earlier that day we would receive the notice of denial for our last chance of obtaining a loan for the pizza shop. Every day at the Academy, I was hoping it would be my last. Heather helped me realize that it must not be God's plan for me and to let it go and appreciate the opportunity He had given me. She was right. I had to stay focused and keep pushing.

Off to the coffee house we went. Shortly after arriving we were asked to help in the cafe during the break. We didn't mind, we were there to help wherever we were needed. While we were in the cafe, close friends of ours asked me if everything was okay. Of course, I was broken on the inside but was trying to keep that to myself. I nodded yes everything is good and kept working. During clean up at the end of the night the same couple invited Heather and I to the local 24-hour diner for a snack.

Jamie and Catherine, the reason why my dreams came to fruition.

I got to know the O'Hara's through church and their son Brad. We became friends after going to youth group and started hanging out outside of church. Before long they were my second family. I would spend more time there than my own home. Through the years, Jamie and Catherine would keep connected with me and often talked to me about God. I admired how much both of them loved God and each other. They became great role models for Heather and me. They even threw us an engagement party and took our pictures at our wedding. Just simply an amazing couple.

So here we are at the diner chatting it up. Out of the blue, Catherine says "we asked you out here tonight because God laid it on our hearts to help you with whatever it was that you're struggling with." They heard God's voice and wanted to do what they could to help us. I honestly couldn't believe what I was hearing. We started talking about my chance to own my own pizza shop. Unfortunately, I explained I couldn't get any banks or institutions to loan me the money. With no hesitation they told me to call the last one we were working with and invite the loan officer to their house for dinner to discuss what was in the way for me to obtain the loan. I was completely stunned.

A few nights later we were having dinner with them and Ms. Rose from The Cooperative Business Assistance Corporation from Camden, New Jersey. Ms. Rose basically just said that Heather and I were young and didn't have enough established credit to obtain the loan. Jamie walked out of the room and returned with a folder of papers. He handed the folder to Ms. Rose and said, "this should help get them whatever they need." "What? Is this real? Am I Dreaming?" This can't be happening. Are you serious? Heather and I were totally speechless. They just handed over a folder that could change the game.

There weren't enough words to describe how grateful I was to them. We wouldn't know for a while what would happen next. So off to that concrete pad for roll call on Monday morning I went. I was committed to finishing the Academy unless God had a different plan. Within a few days we got the news, God had a different plan for us. They approved my loan with the O'Hara's help. I couldn't believe that God had answered my prayers, I didn't even know which way to turn.

There was so much to do, and I couldn't figure out where to start. First thing was for me to drop out of the police academy, God knew my heart. Apparently, it wasn't meant for me to be a cop. So many emotions were running through my head. I called and told Reds, my boss, that I got a loan and that we wanted to buy his daughter's pizza shop. So much had to be done, boy what a learning experience for me. I was so blessed to have so many knowledgeable people on my side. God was so faithful; He had a plan for my life. Sometimes we just have to be patient and trust in His plan and His timing, not our own.

Chapter 15

IN OVER MY HEAD

So much to get done, all in a very short amount of time. My life changed in an instant. Our settlement date was quickly approaching for the pizza shop. I had no idea so much was involved in getting ready for settlement and our grand opening. Utilities had to be put in our names, I had no clue about the amount of money it would take just to get things changed over to our name. We never planned for this part. I am talking about thousands of dollars. Once again, God showed up. The O'Hara's helped us with a small personal loan to help with utilities. My dad was so kind to help us out too. Heather and I exhausted every little bit of money we had to make this dream come true for us. During the day I would work hard getting everything together for settlement and at night, I would go to the pizza shop and paint and make small changes while they were closed. The owner was so nice to let me come in a few days ahead of settlement to start working on little things that I wanted to change.

Settlement day was upon us. I can remember waking up that morning scared and nervous but excited all at the same time. My time had finally come. Our settlement was scheduled for 11:00 a.m. in Bridgeton, across from the county courthouse. I had never been a part of a settlement for anything in my life. Walking in, my belly was in knots. I just remember seeing all the attorneys, the owners of the shop and settlement officials there. Line by line, we went through the settlement sheet to make sure everything was right. After about an hour's time, I was finally handed the key to my future. Totally excited and nervous at the same time, I quickly turned my energy towards getting the shop ready for opening day the next morning.

I had already lined up a crew of friends and family to come over to the shop and help us get it ready to be open the next day. What a crazy day it was, from painting to scrubbing floors and cleaning all of the equipment, the time flew by. Before I knew it, the crowd had left, and my brother and I were the last two there. Finally, everything was done, and it was only 3:00 a.m. Boy was I tired! I had to be back to get everything ready and open by 11:00 a.m. So, I basically went home, showered, took a nap and got back to the shop by 8:30 a.m. I knew from that day; my life would never be what it once was.

Pizza Queen in its current state. This building has seen plenty of renovations over the last 16 years.

My dream had come true and now I had to do what it took to be successful at it. For the coming days, weeks and even months, the adrenaline is what would sustain me. I was faced with a lot of different obstacles early on. I honestly knew it wasn't going to be easy. My home life was pretty much non-existent, and I found myself just coming home long enough to shower, sleep, do some paperwork early in the morning and run right back and start all over again.

Heather would have to bring Kyleigh over to the shop at night for her to see me. Kyleigh would be sleeping when I left in the morning and back to sleep by the time I got home at night. It was taking a toll on my home life and marriage not long after we opened. Heather and I vowed that we would keep a very open line of communication through it all. Neither one of us was ready for the impact it was having on us as a family.

Heather was working full-time; we had a one-year old child and I was basically never around. You could say Heather was a single mom trying to navigate a new norm. Trust me, it wasn't easy to concentrate on the pizza shop when you knew your home life was falling apart day by day. Don't get me wrong, the shop was doing great. We were making a little money and paying all of our bills. People could look at us from afar and say, "boy they are doing very well." Ironically, we both knew it was only a matter of time before something was going to break. The question was what?

I also found myself putting in way more effort at the shop then with my family. Keep in mind, everything I was doing for the shop was for my family. I knew I had to be successful in order to provide for my family. I told myself from the start, I would do everything in my power to make sure that the shop would be able to give my family a better life than I ever had. I didn't care what I had to do to get the job done. What I didn't realize was that I was slowly losing the family that I was working so hard for. My focus had been so set on being successful, I lost what the true meaning of success really was.

You see, I was basing the idea of success on material things. The pizza shop was providing "things" for us. Little over a year after opening the shop, we were able to buy our first house. Finally, all of my hard work and sacrifice was paying off. Heather had a smile from ear-to-ear although it was temporary. We went out and bought new furniture, and once again I saw that smile. Yet again it was temporary. Time and time again we were able to obtain nice things and do things that we never thought would be possible. I was doing everything in my power to provide for my family.

Finally, one day after working a double I came home and just wanted to eat, take a shower and go to sleep. Heather had different plans. I could see it in her face, she was so sad. It looked as if she had to tell me some bad news. "Did someone die?" I asked, "What's wrong Heather?" She began telling me that she didn't sign up for this. Being alone was not what she had in mind. Getting married was a commitment to spend our lives alongside one another, not going to bed and waking up alone. Being a parent was something she always dreamt about, just never a single parent. With tears streaming down both of our cheeks, we had finally reached our breaking point. Our marriage was officially hanging on by a thread. At that moment it hit me.

I looked her square in the face and told her, "every day I leave, I leave for you. Trust me, I want nothing more than to lay next to you and hold you. However, it's my job to provide for you. Every time I talked to you on the phone and heard what you and Kyleigh were doing or where you guys were going, I would often think about turning off the lights and locking the door at the shop just to hang out with you guys but I have to provide for you. How about all the times I would have to hear about all of Kyleigh's "firsts" that I would miss? Don't think for one minute that you are the only one missing out. The only thing that keeps me going to that shop every day is the fact that I did sign up for something. Something that is worth more to me than life itself. That is, you and that baby girl. My body is hurting along with my mind and heart. However, I have to make every effort I can to continue to provide for my family."

Finally, I said to her "just know this, I would rather be broke in material things and have you guys by my side than to have all the success and money in the world and have no one to share it with." From that day forward, we learned to talk daily. I made changes in the way I handled "life" in general. I adjusted my schedule at work, spent more time with family, and kept our eyes focused on God.

Family time was finally happening for us for the first time since opening the shop. I was blessed to be able to hire more staff and learn to trust other people to do some of what was weighing me down from day to day. Sometimes we just have to hit a low in our lives to make much-needed changes. God had once again blessed our family with another baby girl. Mackenzie Paige Johnson joined our family on February 6, 2007. I think it was God's way of showing us that he was proud of us for not giving up. Maybe even a test to see how we would do things differently this time around. With me having way more help at the shop and having been open for a while, things were definitely going to be different for me as a husband and a dad.

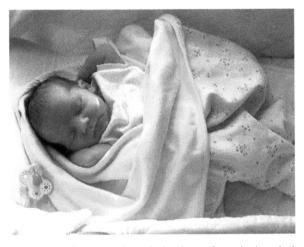

Mackenzie, the day we brought her home from the hospital.

Now we have two daughters, Kyleigh is 3 and our newborn is Mackenzie Paige Johnson who made her debut on February 6, 2007. Things this time around were a little different for us. Still crazy busy, I don't think that will ever change about our family, but definitely a little more mature and grounded as a household. Heather had made a career change right before we purchased our first home and was now working at a local preschool provider as a social worker. I was still doing my thing at the pizza shop. By this time, thank God, I was able to be home much more than in the beginning. I actually started a little side business renting out inflatables on the weekends for kid's parties. Heather was enrolled back in college to get her teaching degree as well. See, I told you things were still busy but definitely more manageable. Heather and I had grown so much as individuals and in our marriage. We knew what we had come through and we thought nothing could stop us now.

Big sister Kyleigh holding Mackenzie the day she came home from the hospital.

Life continued to throw things at us any chance it could. Mackenzie was developing slower than Kyleigh had and we were concerned with the fact that she wasn't walking yet at 14 months old. The doctors warned us not to compare her to Kyleigh. We needed to give her more time. After turning 15 months old she began walking but was falling a lot. Back to the doctors we went and this time the prognosis was a bit different. He watched as Mackenzie waddled around his office falling multiple times. Heather was convinced that one of Mackenzie's legs was longer than the other. The doctor said, "I honestly don't think it's a leg-length discrepancy, I think it has to do with her hip." He referred us to a specialist for further testing.

We took Mackenzie to Nemours DuPont Hospital for Children in the next state over, Delaware. The Orthopedic Specialist we saw, Dr. Mihir Thacker, examined Mackenzie and told us his thoughts immediately but would get an x-ray just to confirm. This doctor was spot-on from his very first examination of Kenz. He explained to us that Kenz was suffering from what's called hip dysplasia on the left side. She was either born this way or it may have happened during delivery. Regardless, she would need to have surgery to repair it. Heather and I were both in disbelief. Heather took the news very hard. She basically passed out in her chair during our conference with the orthopedic doctor. I was upset but knew we had to do what was best for Kenz. The last thing we wanted to hear was that our 19-month-old daughter was going to need to have a major 7-hour surgery to build her left hip socket. We had to rely on God's help to get us through this trying time.

We had no idea what to expect. The hospital was so amazing, they helped get us prepared for pre- and post-surgery. We still had no clue what was in store for us. Before we knew it, it was time to kiss our little baby girl as they carried her off into the operating room. Immediately I broke down into tears and emotions. The fact of the unknown was too much for me to deal with. Up until this time, Heather was the basket case. Well, let me just tell you I made up for it the day of surgery. Seven hours seemed like days to me. All I wanted was to hold my baby girl in my arms. The support and love from all of our friends and family helped us get through that awful day. My staff at the shop also helped out and stepped up in a huge way so I could focus on my family.

We were finally called back into recovery to see our baby girl. Even though we were told what to expect, it didn't hit us until we got back there and saw her. Our world as we know it would not be the same for quite some time. Kenz was sporting a bright pink body cast from her chest all the way down to her ankles. This would be our new normal for a while, about the next three to four months. Kenz wasn't able to walk, use the restroom, or do any of her normal activity that she did prior to the surgery. At only 20 months old, it wasn't easy for her to understand. Heather and I knew it was going to take both of us to do some adjusting but we would get through this together as a family and come out on the other side of this stronger than ever before.

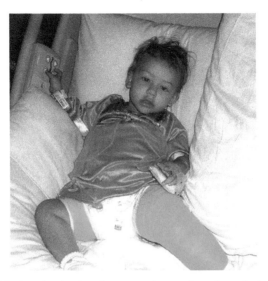

Mackenzie after her first cast change about 6 weeks in, the first cast went to her ankles on both legs leaving her completely immobile.

Believe it or not, Mackenzie did really well. We all did our part and she was able to come out of her cast a little earlier than expected. With tons of intensive physical therapy and continued support, Kenz made a full recovery and is living a normal life and able to do everything all of her peers can do, some even a little better. Life can and will get tough from time to time, that's just the way it is. The difference lies with who it BREAKS and who it MAKES! The saying is true "Only the Strong Survive!"

Chapter 16

THE GOOD, BAD AND UGLY

Throughout the years, some days were better than others. I found myself often working about 70 to 80 hours per week between Pizza Queen and Bouncin' Buddies. Heather was continuing her college career and education. She wanted to finish so she could become a Lead Teacher. She was blessed with an opportunity to become an assistant teacher at the school where she was doing social work. With her goal of becoming a teacher just a few classes away, she thought it would be a good idea to get in classroom experience. From the very first day, she knew it was what she wanted to do. She would work during the day and go to college classes at night, attend online classes and even do some Saturday courses as well. One thing about Heather, when she makes up her mind, she won't stop until she achieves it.

With now having two kids, the pressure would become a bit much once again. This time around things were a little different. I knew she had put all her goals aside while I was doing what I needed to do so the pizza shop could get off the ground. It was time for her to be able to focus on her dreams and aspirations. I juggled things around so I could do everything I had to do with the kids and family life in order for Heather to concentrate, graduate and move on to her career. Honestly, the fact that she was finally pursuing her goals made me feel so blessed to be apart.

Even though I was excited and happy for Heather, in my mind I was freaking out. All I thought about was how I was going to manage everything that needed to be done in a day. From the minute I woke up until the minute I finally fell asleep, something was always on my plate. The pizza shop was growing, which was a blessing and a headache all at the same time. From the very first day, I told myself I would always see every day at the shop like it was my first. I needed to keep that thought in my mind, so I never took it for granted. The busier the store became, the more I realized that I couldn't do it alone. I needed to surround myself with people who shared my same work ethic.

I started to slowly change the way the shop was set up. I knew that it was time to put key people in certain positions to help carry the load and allow me to focus on Bouncin' Buddies and on my family. Don't get me wrong I was still there every day to some capacity. We were open 7 days a week and fed kids Monday through Friday for school lunches. I was able to have a contract with two local private schools to provide lunch for each child every day during the school year. One of the best things I did was bring my mother-in-law in to help with school lunches. She had owned her own catering business for years. Bringing her onboard helped me out tremendously. She primarily focused on the day-to-day operation of school lunches. So much had to take place every morning just to get the doors open. Having hired shift leaders and a manager helped me maintain the pizza shop and allow us to handle growth and become an all-around better shop.

One of the most important people in all of Pizza Queen throughout the years has been Little Mikey. This kid started off with us by coming in on Friday nights with his mom to eat. He would finish his food and ask if he could help out by making pizza boxes. "Free Labor? No problem" I would say. Before long like he was coming in a few times a week just to make boxes. One Friday night his dad happened to walk into the shop while he was still eating with his mom. Shortly after he sat with his family he looked up and said, "Robbie Johnson?" Wow, to my surprise I came to find out that Mikey's dad was my fourth-grade teacher Mr. Devono. No doubt one of my favorite teachers all through school. "Small world," I said as they all finished eating. From that night, we grew closer as friends and their son would start his career in the pizza world.

Mikey and his mom Diane celebrating Christmas with our family.

Mikey has been with me since he was 12 years old. He has grown in so many ways through his time at the pizza shop. From making boxes at age 12, to answering phones, taking orders throughout middle school and finally cooking on the grill through High School. Everything I taught him; he became the best at it. I began to selfishly pray that he would stay with me at the shop after high school and help me keep Pizza Queen at its best. At the same time, I honestly wanted whatever he chose to be his decision.

Throughout the years we became so close he was like my little brother. I knew he would be great at whatever he decided. Fortunately, I am happy to say he is still with Pizza Queen to this day. He manages our daily operations along with another manager Steve Ortiz. I've been blessed to work with a bunch of great people throughout my 16 years of owning Pizza Queen. Some that I had worked with in the early years of Big John's and some that I just hired and trained myself.

Owning a small business is no little task. Some days it will make you want to throw in the towel and walk away. I know I went through plenty of those days. The days that stick with you most are those really bad ones that you wish never took place. I can remember finding out that both my grandparents died on separate occasions while I was at work. See, most people think that just because you're the owner, you can just turn the lights off and tend to life as it comes. Let's just say it's not that easy. The only way you can pay bills is by being open! If you don't open, you can't make money. I didn't have sick days, compensation time or vacation time to take. Actually, I received numerous phone calls throughout the years about family and friends passing. Unfortunately, I never just ran out. I would always work the day or night out and then take care of my family.

One Tuesday morning changed that a little for me though. I remember getting a call at the shop around 10:00 a.m. before the store opened for the day. I usually don't answer calls that early, that day I did for some reason. As I picked up and said "Hello, Pizza Queen," I hear this voice ask if this was Rob? I said, "What's up Pat?" It was my stepmom on the other end. She replied, "your dad died this morning." "Wait, what?" I responded. She began telling me that my dad suffered a massive heart attack while at work. I was in total disbelief.

I grabbed my keys and drove down to Heather's school and asked them to have her come outside. They knew something wasn't right. The moment Heather saw me sitting in the truck, she said "who died?" I went on to tell her my dad suffered a massive heart attack that morning. She immediately wanted to drive up to North Jersey to be with his wife and the rest of the family. Once again, I thought about the shop. I know I had to open by 11 that morning.

She left work to come be with me. She found help to come to the shop and got her mom to grab the kids so we could go see my dad's wife and help in any way we could. I couldn't wrap my head around the fact that he was gone. I just talked to him the night before. He called to talk while I was at work. I always tried to talk anytime we could however, that night was kind of busy and I had to cut our conversation short. Who would have ever thought it would have been the very last time we spoke? I was blessed to have been able to know him for 10 years. He definitely became one of my best friends and I will always be grateful for the time we shared. Love you always Poppop Clown Nose, as Kyleigh and Mackenzie always referred to him.

After running the shop for six or seven years, you could start to see the growth. We were finally getting past the "First Five-Year struggles" as they say. I think it's more like a seven to eight-year struggle. At least that's what it felt like to me. I'm sure I'm my worst critic though. Tough decisions are always being put in front of you. Coming from my background, I had to be very careful with every decision I made. Every dollar counted; every bad decision could put me that much closer to locking my doors for good. I didn't have "net" to fall back on. My parents weren't there to fix my mistakes. However, I also knew that in order to be the best you have to be willing to take risks. I like to call them smart risk even though a risk is a risk.

At this point, after starting Pizza Queen with only $21 in our bank account, I knew we couldn't lose. I proved to myself that I had what it takes to be successful and make good rational decisions. Our inflatable business was picking up and I wanted to expand our equipment so we could begin doing school functions and big community events. We went from just three small bouncy units to over 20 pieces in just over a year's time. The crew at the pizza shop was doing great and enabled me to focus on the bouncy business on the weekends. Things were going so well. God was truly blessing us.

Before long, we were contracted with local municipalities to do their Community Days and just about every school near us for school events. I found myself complaining at times about how busy I was. I never had any time to do anything. I would also have to remind myself that this is what I had asked for. Don't get me wrong, hard work pays off. Heather and I were blessed to be able to provide for our family and have things that we weren't able to have growing up. One of the things that we had in mind was getting a bigger house. We had outgrown our first home and were finally financially in a position to look for a new house.

Heather had big aspirations, me on the other hand, knew we what could afford and stuck around the budget. Heather would have us riding around for hours at a time looking for the right spot. One day she got the bright idea to go ride around the east side of Vineland, an area that was definitely out of our price range. I couldn't tell her anything. She had an idea and was willing to exhaust every option in the meantime. She was going off of a list on her phone of all the available properties in the area. Nothing had really caught our eye, definitely nothing in our price range.

As I'm driving out of our last development of the day, Heather yells "oh, go back! I saw a sign down that road." So, me being a good husband, turned around and went down the street where she saw the sign. The whole time, I'm laughing "these houses are huge! We could never afford any of these!" She responds "ye of little faith." As we pull into the driveway she says, "Yeah maybe you're right, we can't afford this house!" We get out anyway and look around because, why not? We are already here. We peaked in the windows and went around back. "It looks like it needs a lot of work" we agreed. As we were getting back in the car Heather says, "let's call to see how much it's listed for just because." At this point I'm like "whatever, call the number."

The realtor answered and said he could meet us there in about an hour but never talked price. Talk about giddy, Heather was freaking out. I explained to her not to get her hopes up because "this is way too much for us and you know it." We took a ride and looked at more houses and then it was time to go back. As we pulled back up in the driveway, the front door was wide open. We walked in and thought "what are we getting ourselves into?"

The house was big, and all torn up. The realtor explained that it was a foreclosure and the people just destroyed it before leaving. When I say it was bad, I mean bad as in huge holes in the walls, black stains on all the carpets, vulgar sayings written in black marker all over the walls, sheet rock missing, no railings on the steps, doors off the hinges, no knobs on any of the cabinets or drawers, missing appliances, and so much more. I honestly couldn't believe what I was looking at. One thing about me, kind of like the pizza shop, you have to see things for what they can be, not always their value when you see it.

Heather struggled to see what the house could be. To our surprise, with it being a foreclosure, it wasn't far off from what we were looking to pay. Before leaving the realtor said "if you even remotely like what you saw, you need to put a bid in today. A lot of people have been looking at it." We thanked him for showing up and drove away. Here I am again thinking about the whole risk and reward mindset. Heather feels defeated already and just thinks it's too much for us to take on. We have overcome so much together; this would just be another part of our success story. Who would have thought that at the time? After talking about what the house could be, I said to Heather, "let's just put in an offer," and without hesitation she called and started the process of putting in our bid.

We told God from the start, if it was His will for us, it would happen. We became a part of a bidding war situation. At the end of it all, we won and were asked to come sign all the paperwork. During the process of signing, we noticed the amount was $5,000 more than what we agreed upon. We assured the realtor it was wrong, and we wanted it changed. He said if he changed the price it would go back into the bidding war and most likely we would lose our chance. We said we were willing to take that chance.

After leaving, feeling frustrated and defeated, we prayed that God would intervene on our behalf. If it was meant to be it would be. The following day we were contacted that the house would go back to the other bidders. We were very upset but felt that it was just not meant to be. We had already had our hearts set on the new house so you can imagine our disappointment. God had different plans. That's all we kept telling ourselves, so we didn't go nuts.

Two days later we get the call that the other buyers fell through financially and the bank would accept our offer. The $5,000 less offer that should have been on the contract in the first place. We couldn't believe it. God had heard us and gave us the desires of our heart. We just had to be patient and allow Him to work it out. With tons of family and friends helping us day and night we were able to transform that dilapidated broken down house into our dream home within 10 days. What a difference we were able to make in such a short time. God had truly blessed us.

Turns out, He had actually blessed us in more ways than one. Within that next year, we found out we were pregnant with our third child. We were not expecting to get pregnant. Heather and I had talked about me getting fixed. We were content with our two girls. I actually had a consultation date set with a local urologist when Heather found out she was pregnant.

Heather didn't take the news too well. She actually found out one day before her birthday, not exactly what she was expecting. We had not long before moved into our Dream House, Heather was in her master's program for teaching, and things were finally starting to settle. It honestly took some time before we could get excited about this one. At this point, we thought the whole kid thing was done for us. It took a lot of prayer for us as a couple to understand and be okay with the gift that God was giving us. Not our proudest parenting moments but it's the honest truth.

We had to remind ourselves that everything happens for a reason. God doesn't make mistakes; we were chosen by God to raise another child. Once we changed our focus, we began to understand and accept the fact that we were going to be parents to a newborn all over again. It became such a happy time for our family. The fact that we were having a boy this time changed the game for both of us. They say, "the third time's a charm," well that couldn't be truer. On March 28, 2014 we brought Dallas Michael Johnson into this world. He definitely changed our lives for the better the moment he made his debut. He continues to be our daily dose of joy from the Lord. Remember, God knows best regardless if you understand or not, just have faith!

Dallas Michael Johnson shortly after delivery weighing in at 8lbs 10ozs

Dallas has grown so quickly. He is truly a gift from God and exactly what we needed to complete our family.

Chapter 17

LEGENDS LOST

No one ever wants to think about losing someone close to you. As you get older, it seems to happen more and more. Throughout my life there were so many great people who helped mold and shape me into the man I am today. I wish I honestly didn't have a reason to even write a chapter like this. Unfortunately, God had a different plan. I'm continuously told to just trust Him.

I still remember the day I got the call from one of my good friends, more like a big brother to me. He called and said, "I would come visit mom soon she doesn't have long." Without hesitation I called my life-long friend Shelton and told him about the situation. Shelton lives in Maryland and I knew he would definitely want to say his goodbyes as well. The following day we were able to meet at my mentors' house. His wife Alice was like a second mother to us growing up. She was our choir director, a youth group leader and our boss's wife. She was such a sweet woman. She would always put others before herself. I even had the pleasure of working with her from time to time.

She had been diagnosed with a brain tumor. Such sad news for all of us who love her. Alice was such a strong woman of faith. Regardless of the outcome, she had told us she was winning either way. Within days of our visit, she lost her fight on Earth and earned her wings in Heaven with Jesus. She would always say "to be absent from the body means to be present with the Lord." Even though she wasn't suffering anymore, it was difficult to watch my mentor try to carry on. His life became so different. It was like he lost his purpose in life. As we would continue to visit and stay in touch, he would often tell me he missed his best friend. Throughout all of my years knowing Reds, I never quite saw him this sad. It honestly broke my heart.

Reds and his wife Alice before the health issues.

We would continue to talk often, mostly about pizza stuff. I always valued his opinion on everything in life, he always had the right things to say to me. Not long after his wife's passing, Red's started to not feel too well himself. One Sunday afternoon, he drove to get payroll for the pizza shop, a long-time regimen of his for Sunday afternoons. While coming home, he passed out and ran off the road into some bushes. That was the beginning of his downward health prognosis.

He was in and out of the hospital a few times due to heart issues. Right in front of my very eyes, I was watching my mentor, the strongest most knowledgeable God-fearing man I've ever known, grow tired, weak and sick. He began to lose weight from loss of appetite. You could tell he had lost his reason for living anymore. Losing his wife was just too much for him to bear. Through his sickness and time he had left, he would tell anyone who would listen about his "Savior." I would try to spend as much time with him as I possibly could. I could never get enough knowledge from him. Every word he spoke was something I could use in life.

One day while visiting him in the rehab, he began to talk about our journey throughout the years and the pizza business. He couldn't believe how far I'd come. He began to speak about how hundreds upon hundreds of people had come through his doors throughout his career. Some would just stay for a little while, while others stayed around for years. "No matter how long they lasted at the shop" he said, "I would try to teach anyone who would listen." He told me after all the years that he could probably fit into one hand those that took his advice. I'll never forget that moment he grabbed my hand and said, "you're one of those who listened". As tears began to roll down our cheeks, I leaned into the bed to give him a hug to leave. His last words to me that I will never forget come out of his mouth were, "I'm glad I didn't waste my time on you!"

One of the last deep conversations I would have with my mentor Reds.

It wasn't long after that I would receive a phone call from his son yet again, this time telling me that my "GOAT" had passed that morning. I couldn't believe what I was hearing, I had plans to visit him that afternoon. Once again, God had a different plan. My life, my career, my tomorrow had just been changed forever. Words cannot describe my gratitude towards this awesome human being. I work so hard day to day to try to be half the man he was. I was honored to be chosen to speak on behalf of his life and legacy at his funeral.

Below is how I best tried to describe how much he meant to me. These are the actual words I spoke that day in 2014:

"I was asked to speak at Red's home going service. It was the hardest thing I've ever done. There will never be another human like him. Reds taught me so much through the years. More than anything else, he taught me to love the Lord and trust Him no matter what. Our relationship started when I was only 11 years old, right here in this church. I was brought here as a "van kid" and ended up being a kid adopted by many families of this church including the Scott family. I used to beg Reds every Sunday for a job. His response was always the same. "Your turn will come." One Saturday morning there was a knock at the door, very early I might add. The crazy part is that I wasn't even at my house. I was staying at Bob & Pauline Smith's house. They had invited me to stay over and go to Cape May with them. I get to the door and Reds says, "It's your turn, you ready?" I explained my plans of going to Cape May and he asked me if I was gonna get paid for going to Cape May. My response was,

"I'll be right back, don't leave, I'm going with you."

From that very day, my life has never been the same. Boy was he trying to break me; he dropped me off at the Vineland store with Reggie, Renei and Alice. And to top it all off, my first job was chopping onions, my least favorite job to this day! I made it through the day and plenty of other days like it. Thinking back now, he was just preparing me for my future. Throughout my time at Big John's our relationship changed. He began to take on other roles in my life. Doing things that didn't even pertain to the shop. He cared about my mom having enough money to pay our rent at Tips Trailer Park, oil to heat the trailer and food to eat at the table. He even gave me my first car. I'll never forget it. It was an 87 Mercury Topaz, baby blue. He set me up on payments that had to be paid before I could have the car. When I gave him the last payment, he handed me an envelope of money and said, "now you have enough money to insure it." He was always a step ahead to make sure you got what you needed.

It wasn't always happy times that we shared. He had to deal with me in all types of situations. Believe it or not, I was young and hardheaded at times. But no matter what I did, his advice and timing was always perfect. Sometimes I listened, and sometimes I didn't. There were times I quit on him, some days I didn't even show up at all. No matter what the case, he never gave up on me. He would tell me that he was praying for me and he always welcomed me back with open arms. I have witnessed so many things that Reds has done to bless others. He showed me the true meaning of God's love for others. He taught me how to love people!

When I was asked if I wanted to speak today, I knew I wanted to honor him in any way possible. I began to think of words to describe the person he was courageous, dependable, ambitious, loving, generous, wise, joyful, obedient, pleasant, hardworking, sincere, the list goes on. But after looking through all these words to describe him, I realized that the one word that sums up what he was to me was HERO! There will never be another one like him. I can only pray that I can be half the man he was. I will be forever grateful to have had him as a part of my life!

After his passing, word spread like wildfire on social media. Tons of people were remembering him for what they knew him for, the icon of pizza! I had made up my mind that I wasn't going to post anything. Then I realized that most of the people posting were reminiscing about the works of his hands. I felt led to write my story about the works of his heart. Here's what I wrote.

"Where do I start, what do I even say?" I have been thinking about the right thing to say and can't even find a word that describes how I feel. I lost one of the most influential men in my life. I'm really lost for words. He wore so many hats in a day's time and was great at them all. He was a man with great wisdom, compassion and had a heart filled with love for everyone around him. I don't know where my life would be without the guidance and love that he showed me. This quote from him to me will forever remain in my heart. He said, "Son, I'm so glad I didn't waste my time on you!" Reds you are and always will be my HERO. Til we make

> pies in the sky together my friend, I love
> and miss you Reds! ~ Rob Johnson

They say death seems to happen in threes. I'm not one for believing wise fables such as that however, within a year's time or so I lost three very important people in my life. The whole "death happens in threes" came true.

Throughout my career at Big John's Pizza, I worked with a lot of guys that I would learn the trade from. One of my all-time favorites was Rich Keener. That guy always made you smile and have a good time even when you were busy and going crazy. Rich's smile was contagious. Over the years, our lives went different ways. Eventually Rich ended up leaving the pizza business and became a custodian for a local school in our area. After buying Pizza Queen and my life spiraling out of control, God allowed Rich and my paths to meet again. As we were reminiscing about all the good times, he mentioned he had some free time if it would help me out at the pizza shop. He offered to come work part-time for me to help me free up and gain a little control on my personal life. His offer couldn't have come at a better time.

Rich with his granddaughter Ella who often visited him at the shop when he was working.

From the very first day he walked into Pizza Queen it just felt right. He would continue to work every other Saturday for years to come. If I needed a different day off for any reason, Rich would try his hardest to help me out. It was definitely a God thing. The coolest part about him working for me was that my girls called him "Uncle Rich", that was what I grew up working at Big John's calling him too. It kind of went full circle.

Rich always wanted to be busy while at the shop. He hated just standing around. His motto was "if you have time to lean, you have time to clean." Throughout the year certain days and holidays were busier than others. Rich was always ready to step in and help me anytime I needed him. Halloween is always a very busy day for us at the shop. Rich looked forward to Halloween, this Halloween was just a little different for us. Rich started his shift that Saturday a little later than usual because I knew we were going to get rocked and I wanted him to be well rested for the rush at dinner. The night didn't disappoint, we were crazy busy. Rich however didn't seem like himself. He was definitely a little off. Not thinking anything of it I sent him home early. He looked tired and a little confused.

The following day I followed up with a phone call. To my surprise, his wife had to take him to the hospital for shortness of breath and dizziness. The news only got worse. Rich had been diagnosed with lung cancer. It honestly was so devastating to hear. Rich started to decline by the day and his lungs were not good. They had just given him months to live.

Rich also taught Sunday school and went to church every Sunday. He knew that God would have the final say. He kept the faith through it all. My heart broke every time I would visit him. You could see more and more of the devastation this ugly monster was doing to this gentle, loving, happy, kind-hearted soul.

The night before Jesus called Rich home, all the guys at the pizza shop went up after work to see him. We stayed with him well into the morning hours not knowing if it would be our last visit with him here on Earth. It was so hard to say goodbye each time we visited. As we took turns hugging him and saying goodbye, he lifted his head up and smiled. His last words to me were, "it's not goodbye it's see you later!"

That year was really hard to understand. I couldn't wrap my head around the fact that I lost three very important people in my life. My faith in God is the only thing that helped me get through it. As time goes by, it becomes a little easier. Now I look back and realize that everything happens for a reason. We don't always understand however, you learn to be grateful for the time you had. These three awesome people each played a role in helping me become the man I am today. I will never forget the impact they had on my life. They continued to believe in me during the times I didn't even believe in myself. Don't forget where you came from and those who helped you get there. Always pay it forward!

I will leave you with this, "The greatest good you can do for another is not just to share your riches but to reveal to him his own." (Benjamin Disraeli)

Chapter 18

YOU JUST NEVER KNOW

It was quite different around the shop after the passing of Uncle Rich. During my time working at Big John's I became friends with Rich's nephew Steve who was a little younger than me. I was there the first day he started. Steve pretty much started off his career in the pizza shop quite like I did. I got to see him work himself right up the ranks. He was actually part owner with his Uncle Rich at the Vineland Big John's when I purchased Pizza Queen. I can remember walking into the shop there to give them the news of me opening up Pizza Queen. I wish I could say either of them were happy for me. It was actually the total opposite. Steve, who had become a pretty close friend, told me he felt betrayed. With our pizza shops only being miles apart, he felt I may hurt his business. I was trying to explain there was enough to go around. Unfortunately, he didn't take it that way. Who would have thought it would be the last time I would speak to him until the funeral of our Mentor Reds.

About 12 years had gone by. Not long after the funeral, one Friday night Steve walked into the shop to grab a pizza and talk. It was honestly great to be able to catch up with him. During our conversation he began telling me all this horror about him at his pizza shop. He eventually became full-time owner with his parents and family's help. He lasted a few years, after about having a nervous breakdown he realized he didn't want the headache anymore. He sold out and moved on with his life. He told me if I ever needed help to hit him up. I took his number for a rainy day. Months later was when Steve's Uncle Rich, who was working for me from time to time, became ill. This left a hole in the schedule at the shop.

That rainy day had finally come, I called Steve and asked if he would be available during the times needed. To my surprise, within a few days Steve was in my shop tossing pies. Talk about full circle, I couldn't believe what I was seeing. Watching him behind the counter just felt right. It was even cooler to know he was in Uncle Rich's spot.

The pizza shop was continuing to grow daily. With Mikey old enough now to help run the daily operations, I was able to dip and dab in new ideas. For years now, it had been Pizza Queen and Bouncin' Buddies. I don't really understand but I would always tell Heather that I felt like three was the magic number. She would always respond, "you barely have time to sleep as it is." She wasn't lying, but it felt like I had to make a move to secure my future. Being a self-employed person meant that I had to plan for retirement myself. I'm not privileged to have a pension or anything to help once I retire. It was all up to me.

I would talk to different people and do my own research to see what would work best for me. After months of research and looking for what was next, I felt led in my heart to try my hand at real estate. This idea would cost quite a bit of money upfront therefore, it couldn't be something I would just rush into. I would spend tons of time in prayer wanting to make sure it was what I was supposed to be doing. Heather wasn't really on board either. Through our lives, we have learned to trust one another, but mostly we learned to trust God. After coming up with a name for the new business, Heather started to see how intrigued I was and realized she could trust me. I was doing what was needed to be successful. The next day I went to our attorney's office and applied for yet another business license. This time it would be for DMK Management LLC.

I named this company after my three children Dallas, Mackenzie and Kyleigh. Hopefully one day, my kids can continue the business and make dad proud. People would often ask me why real estate? During my time of researching, I couldn't find much of anything else that could potentially pay you like owning rentals. It's definitely not a get-rich-quick scheme, most things aren't. You have to be willing to put in time and money and wait for a return. That's pretty much what a retirement plan is. You put in money all your life so when you finally call it quits, you can still live and earn some money to survive.

Our first deal was really scary to Heather and me. We bid on a quadruplex in our hometown where we both grew up. The scariest part is the 20% down you have to put up for any investment deal. We were able to settle on our very first real estate deal for around $100,000. This was a pretty big deal for two people who are really just getting their feet wet in this real estate world. Two great friends that have knowledge in this field helped us out. Stacy was our agent, she helped us find the right property for just starting out. The property didn't need a lot of work. Also, our commercial loan officer Jason made the whole transaction very smooth for us as well. It definitely isn't what you know, it's who you know. You don't have to know it all, you just have to be willing to learn from those who are around you that are willing to teach you.

I have always said, to be the best, you have to watch and learn from the best. Honestly, real estate has taught me so much in such a short time. Even though you have upfront costs, if you do it right, you should be able to get all your upfront money within four to five years. They say with any business it takes the first five years to start making money. After you get your initial investment back, you will continue to make enough money each month to pay your bills and profit at the same time. Once you get the house paid for, that means more monthly income for the business (you). Let's go one step further, if you finally decide to retire, you can put the property up for sale and make all that profit too. It's honestly a great way to prepare for your future.

I had already opened Roth IRA's and started college funds for the kids. I just felt like I needed to do a little more to secure a future for Heather and me. My advice to you is to never depend on anyone or anything, make it happen for you. They always say if it looks too good to be true, it usually is. While I was reaching another goal, I set for myself, trouble in Paradise was brewing at the pizza shop.

My manager at the time was going through personal problems at home. He began to show up drunk and had to be sent home. With me having a big heart, I would listen to all his problems and give him another chance. I am known for seeing the best in people. At times it would cause me to have problems with other employees, some of which were family. My mother-in-law was one of them. She was always calling a spade a spade. She would often not like my choices of the way I would do things. Neither one of us could win. It was always a fine line between us at the shop. In one way she was my employee but at the same time she was Heather's mom. From time to time we would have disagreements until this one day. This day was different and came out of nowhere. My manager that would cause conflictions at times was there with us working. Something came up between the two of them and I was there to make it right. I felt I had to do what was right for the business and my mother-in-law felt like I chose my manager over her and that I disrespected her. She would leave that morning, throwing her store credit card and key on the counter. I was totally devastated and kind of confused. It was never my intention to hurt her in any way. I was just trying to be fair and do what was best for the business. Shortly after that blow up, I was put in a difficult position once again, this time having to fire my own brother.

One thing I learned, working with family is not a good choice when you are the owner. I'm happy to say that after time went by, I was able to apologize and talk it out with both of them. We all realized the best thing we did was not work together anymore. It was really devastating to not only lose family members, but now to find help to try to fill these openings at the shop. Never an easy task to do. The workforce is slim pickings to say the least. All I could do is pray and let God do His thing.

My aunt, who worked for me when I first opened, thought about coming back after being gone for years. I had to fill these open spots so here I go again hiring family. The one good thing about family is that they would always keep an eye on the place. Within a few weeks to a month, things were finally getting back to normal once again. Well, at least I thought that's what was happening. Remember things happen in threes, right?

One Saturday night, I was actually away, I get a phone call around 10:30 p.m. Mikey was calling to tell me the register was $60 off. He said the manager had left for the night. I went through all the possible ways to help him find the mistake over the phone. After an hour or so, I finally just said to bag up all the paperwork and I would go through it when I got back. Around 1:30 a.m. my phone rings again this time being my manager. He began by saying that Mikey had called him about the money, he went on to tell me that he had taken it. He explained that he met one of the delivery drivers out back at the end of the night and took it from them but kept it in his pocket instead of the register. It was the driver's delivery bank that he started with at the beginning of his shift.

Come to find out, alcohol wasn't his only problem. He had to take it so he could pay his dealer off so they wouldn't destroy his house or him personally. Wow is all I could say. I couldn't believe my ears. It instantly put me in a dark place in my mind as this guy had been with me for years. I taught him the business from the ground up. I stuck with him through so much. I would help with Christmas and birthdays for his kids and so much more. I couldn't believe that he would do this to me. All I could do was think of ways that I could beat my $60 out of him. I felt so betrayed. After talking to him I decided it was best for my family to just return home.

In the middle of the night, here I am driving home with thoughts of what I was going to do to him. To be honest, I thought about taking my gun and going to his house and shooting him that night. I wish I could say I'm lying. Thank God for my wife and another great friend. I was able to discuss it with them both. They made me realize it was the best thing that could have happened to me. It was $60 that night, it could have gone on to become so much more.

This moment in my life was a great test of my faith, I truly failed. I couldn't believe I let this get me so fired up that I was willing to throw everything away for $60. My wife reminded me that "vengeance is mine sayeth the Lord." I was to give it to God and let go. It wasn't what I wanted to hear but definitely what I needed to hear. God showed up in the middle of the storm. Within a few hours I went from wanting to take a life, to praying for him to find Jesus and be healed from his addictions.

What a gaping hole that left at the shop. I always live knowing that a phone call could change my life from day-to-day with the shop. However, I never saw this coming. Things were working so well, almost too good to be true. I have to say Mikey and I put our heads together, prayed and waited on the Lord. The next few months would be quite challenging but good for me. Good things come to those who wait. God had blessed me with a tremendous business, and I knew He would provide in His time.

One morning I woke up with my buddy Steve on my mind. I knew he was working somewhere full-time but felt led to call and discuss him maybe coming to work at Pizza Queen as a manager full time. Currently, he had just been filling in at the shop on Saturdays in his Uncle Rich's spot. After discussing a few details and seeing what his thoughts were, he told me to give him a few days. Within those few days I prayed for God's will to be done. If it was meant to be, allow it to be spoken into existence. My prayer was answered, and Steve became our full-time manager along with Mikey. Those two guys work so hard and Pizza Queen continues to be very successful because of their efforts along with the rest of our staff.

"Meeting of the Minds" is what my wife called this picture when she captured it however, this is a quite normal behind the scenes photo of what we do daily. You have to reflect to grow!

Chapter 19

BE THE CHANGE

They always say that change should start with you. It is so easy to blame others for the things that just aren't right. Sooner or later you have to man up and see how you can make a difference. Once our lives got back to what we considered manageable, I began to focus on ways I could help change the world around me. As God continued to bless me, I wanted to pass the blessings along to others. There are so many ways to make a difference. God has given all of us gifts and it's up to us how we use them. Myself personally, I have always had a heart to help others. I tend to root for "the underdogs" and try to lend a hand when needed. So many times, people often forget where they come from and how they got there.

I know my success has been given to me by God, and I am to use my success as a platform to help others reach their full potential. I find myself daily taking calls, returning emails and texts from people who need help with what's next in life for them. I wish I had all the answers they were looking for however, most cases that is not how it goes down. The upside to that is I never just say I don't know. I will answer them by saying "let me find out." I will work to find them an answer, regardless of how difficult it may become. Most people just need a little encouragement and guidance. It's nice to have somebody you can trust on your side, fighting with you. Most of my life, that was the case for me.

In my mind I always thought about running for a political position so I could fight for those who couldn't fight for themselves. Every year something would come up or I would honestly just be too busy with life to even consider running. With Pizza Queen now having two awesome managers and a great staff, Heather finally graduating with several degrees and working as a teacher, things seemed to line up.

One day, without hesitation, I drove to our county office building and got a petition to run for county free-holder. I chose to run for county office for the simple fact that I had friends and family all around my county who needed a voice. From day one, I went in as an independent candidate. My feelings were more about the people than the party. My opinion on politics is simple, when one certain party wins, more people lose between the opposite party and those stuck in the middle. Most party lines find themselves chasing agendas rather than what's best for the majority.

My first goal was to get the petition signed by enough registered voters to get on the ballot. For the most part, that was the easiest task throughout the election campaign. Within days of obtaining the petition, I was able to return it full of signatures that were needed. Once turned in and all the names were verified it was off to the races. With growing up in different parts of the county, I felt good about reaching out to friends, family and associates to help get the word out. There I was, first timer, pretty much doing it all by myself trying to figure this thing out.

I was told by most people I met that it is impossible to get elected without running with a party. I knew what they were saying was true, but I couldn't choose one side or the other. Both sides had good and bad and then there was that thought about just doing what was right. Ultimately, the fact that somebody needed to stand up for what was right regardless of agendas or party lines, I found myself stuck right in the middle alone. I didn't care that I was the only independent candidate running. From day one, I was out to make history and get a win for the everyday person.

From yard signs to t-shirts, I was handing those bad boys out. My slogan was "Be the Change." I remembered back to my roots, if you want to see change, it has to start with you. Everywhere I would go, that would be my message. Change can and will happen as long as you start it off. If we all do our little part, great things will begin to happen. I often think of a puzzle piece, pretty much useless and boring alone, not much for it to accomplish but when the pieces fit together, and the puzzle is finally complete it becomes a masterpiece. Think about how it starts out, one single piece!

Before long you start adding more and more pieces to it. That's how change happens. All it takes is one idea with dedication and perseverance.

I also thought about my color scheme in order for it to have meaning behind it as well. Most politicians say what people want to hear during an election regardless of how they truly feel. They like to call it the "gray area." That's kind of like staying neutral, that way they can swing a little to the left or right and not be off by much. My campaign was pretty bold from the beginning. I went with the black and white color scheme. I'm personally about telling the truth exactly how I feel. The general public I think would appreciate that approach much better.

My family all ready to hit the campaign trails with me.

I spoke directly on matters with a simple yes or no, agree or disagree decision. Things that matter to voters should be black or white, no gray area! My campaign was a little bit different from the ordinary, I wanted to reflect on who I was as a person. Throughout the few months campaigning, I held numerous Town Hall meetings, tons of public appearances at local events and even hosted a county wide Family Skating event. Getting to meet and talk to all the county residents was the best part of the whole thing.

The Democrats and Republicans also had great people running on their cards that year as well. As November drew near, election day was just around the corner. The final push to get my name and message out there was a night and day job. I couldn't leave one stone unturned. Radio ads were running, my face was in all of our local papers and signs were everywhere in the county. People from all over the county were excited to be able to vote for someone that was going to fight for what's right.

November 2nd had finally arrived, not quite the way I was anticipating though. We had planned a big campaign party at Pizza Queen the night of the election for all those who had been rooting for me throughout the election. The whole event was planned, a tent was set up outside with a menu and entertainment as well. Unfortunately, due to rain and high winds, we could not follow through with our evening as planned. What a complete wreck to what I thought was an amazing campaign. All is never lost in my mind; I always think outside the box. Within a few minutes of me figuring out that our plan could not happen, I was on the phone with hopes of a plan B.

Friends of ours had opened up an inside entertainment place where kids could have birthday parties. I knew it had plenty of room and even a separate place for people to eat. Without hesitation they agreed to let me take the whole night inside. God showed up even in the midst of a storm yet again. You couldn't even tell it wasn't meant to happen there from the beginning. There was plenty of room for the DJ and for dancing, food and seating was plentiful as well. Towards the end of the night as results were going to be coming in, we set up our projector so everyone could watch.

Most of the night I was as calm as I could be. I found myself dancing, eating and just enjoying the company of all who showed up to support me. When that projector went up and the results were live, my whole inner being just got really nervous, to the point of being nauseous. That is not how I usually handle myself in stressful situations. I couldn't believe that the time had finally arrived. As I began to stand around with the crowd watching, I saw my name appear. Showtime, it wouldn't be long before I knew my fate. It honestly didn't matter to me about winning or losing at that point, I was just proud of myself for stepping out of my comfort zone and standing up for what I thought was right.

Final results were in and as most people had told me from the start, it would be impossible for me to win. They were absolutely right as I came in at the bottom of the pack. The fact that I ran my campaign with integrity and kept roots of who I truly am, it felt like a win to me. My supporters were very surprised to see my last place finish but as I spoke for the very last time that night as a candidate I explained, "We may have lost the opportunity for me to be a county freeholder, but we still have an opportunity to be the change as individuals. We may not be able to change the whole world, but you have the power to change your world!"

Chapter 20

THROUGH IT ALL

One day you will get to look back at your life and realize you survived it all. I celebrated my fortieth birthday this past year. When they say, "age is just a number, you're only as old as you feel," I truly feel 40 LOL. So much has happened in these forty years. Regardless of the hurt and pain I may have suffered and endured throughout my life, I have equally experienced happiness and moments of joy that I will cherish till the day I expire.

I have learned that your perspective has a lot to do with your success. As you read through my story, I could have chosen to use a number of issues in my life as a crutch, to give up on life. However, I chose to use each and every opportunity as motivation to keep pushing for a better tomorrow. Take the fact of me being adopted for example. I've come across young people who grow up mad at the world because they were either adopted or raised by someone other than their parents. I can understand why they would feel that way, but my perspective has always been a little different.

I love to share my thoughts and explain a different point of view to them. I explain it this way; I think most parents who give their children up for adoption should be commended. It has to be one of the most unselfish acts a parent could do for their child. You have to see it through the parent's eyes. They have to come to grips that they just aren't fit to do the job right, so they have to find someone more fit to do the job. I'm sure for a mother who carries a child inside of them for 9 months, it's not such an easy process for them.

Being adopted has always made me feel special. I always called myself the chosen one of the family. I would often tell my sister and brother, "mom got stuck with y'all, she had a choice and still chose to bring me home." Almost like being picked from a litter. Think about it like this, when going out for a team at school they would line up all the kids up and have team captains pick their teammates. I don't know about you but every time my name was called, it made me feel pretty special. Since I was old enough to understand the process of adoption, I truly felt special like I got picked for the home team.

I could have easily been left for the system to raise me; however, I was chosen to be a part of a special family that allowed me to become one of them. Perspective changes the game. Throughout my whole life, the fact that I chose to stay motivated allowed me to become the man I am today. Speaking of today, I am happy to say God has been good to our family of

5 and we are all doing very well. My first-born Kyleigh is now 16 years old, and a junior in high school. She'll be getting her license in a few months. I'm not ready for this next chapter of my life. I have a few gray hairs with her name on them but wouldn't change who she is and how God has made her.

Our middle daughter Mackenzie is now 13. She just entered those dreadful teenage years. I have to say she's a very sweet young woman. We like to call her the "old soul" of the kids. She is way beyond her years. All of her medical issues with her hip are doing very well and she is enjoying a normal life now as a teenager.

Dallas is now six, full of life and keeping us young. From the age of 1 ½ to 5, we had some scary medical issues develop including a diagnosis of asthma and epilepsy, but God is all we can say! He is now a kindergartener, yes, we have a high school junior, a 7th grader and a kindergartner. We feel the same as you, "What were they thinking?" Honestly God knows best, our family is perfect and blessed by Him.

Heather continues to teach full-time during the day and also teaches a college course one night a week. Her most important and hardest job by far has to be a mother and a wife. We have come so far in our relationship over the past 22 years. We are coming up on 18 years of marriage. God has truly blessed our union. One of the most important things to remember when it comes to life is this, number one God, second family, the rest will follow. Honor God and take care of your family and your life will be blessed.

As for yours truly, life is awesome but very busy. Most of the time, I run out of hours in the day to finish what I set myself up to do. It's fine though, God has blessed me and would never allow me to have more than I can handle. See it's all about perspective, I could complain but I choose to appreciate the fact that I'm busy. Pizza Queen is in its 16th year of business and continues to break records year after year. Our two awesome managers, Mikey and Steve are still there doing a phenomenal job. At this time, we are serving two local schools their lunch Monday through Friday before we even open up for regular pizza shop business. We serve almost 400 kids every day. Pizza Queen has been blessed to have such an amazing staff to help continue the business to grow year after year.

DMK, LLC, our real estate business, is doing well and continues to grow year after year. We are proud to have over 20 rentals at this time. We are in the midst of hiring office staff to help with the loads of paperwork that comes with owning this type of business. Don't miss out, do your homework and try to obtain some real estate for yourself. It's a great way to help prepare for your retirement.

Honestly, God has been so good to me. Throughout it all, my relationship with God continues to grow. Our family is attending Lakewood Chapel in New Jersey and loving it. Heather and I began teaching our youth group within the last year. What an amazing experience we have had so far. Teaching the teens helps keep me young. I have also been serving as a board member of the church for the past year as well. As I look back throughout my life I feel as though God was preparing me daily for a better tomorrow. God continues to provide and make a way no matter what. Everybody has a story, we don't personally get to write a good portion of it, however you get to write your final chapter. I'm still writing mine; Make It Count!

A current family photo during our quarantined Easter 2020.

ABOUT ROB JOHNSON

Husband, father of three and local business owner, Rob was born, raised, and currently resides in Cumberland County, New Jersey. His focus has always been family and he has poured his blood, sweat and tears into every single accomplishment both personally and professionally. Rob was named our Hometown Hero in 2014 among many accolades he's received over the years. Outside of running two full time businesses, Rob serves as an Elder on his church board and is an active community leader. He has never let his past define his future. Follow him on Facebook: Abandoned NoT Broken or on Instagram: @robjohnsonanb to learn more about him and how God has worked in his life.